The Legend of Sleepy Hollow

by Washington Irving, adapted by Jack Neary

In its developmental stage, THE LEGEND OF SLEEPY HOLLOW was produced by Acting Out! Productions, John and Deirdre Budzyna, producers. It was originally workshopped by the Dracut, Massachusetts schools.

Pictured, from the Acting Out! production in Newburyport, MA, 2017:

Front cover
John Manning and Elizabeth Cormier

Back cover:
Katherine Proulx

> *A table and three chairs. Three Gossips sit at the table, sewing. They are MILLY, KATE and EMMA. Emma is significantly younger than her compatriots. Their job in life is to sit around and gossip.*
>
> *Today, they are gossiping about Ichabod Crane, and what "happened" to him. As the play progresses, these ladies will tell the story as it is illustrated onstage.*

MILLY

Well, if you ask me...

KATE

Nobody asked you.

MILLY

Well, if you ask me, somebody done him in.

EMMA

Done him in, like, murdered him?

MILLY

If you ask me...

KATE

Nobody asked you.

EMMA

Everybody at the tavern says it was the Ghost...

MILLY
(dismissing)

Oh, the Ghost...

EMMA

Yes! The Ghost of the Headless Horseman!

MILLY

Whoever done in Mr. Crane might have been a horseman, but he surely had a head! Ichabod Crane was murdered!

KATE

Oh, you're bonkers!

EMMA

But who would murder a nice man like that?

MILLY

How do you know how nice he was? You only been livin' here three weeks.

                    EMMA
Well, he seemed nice at the sociable.

                    MILLY
Seemin' nice and bein' nice is two different animals. Both
kinds of nice can be murdered, you know.

                    KATE
There wasn't no body!

                    MILLY
Since when do you need a body for a murder?

                    KATE
If there's no body, how do you know he's dead?

                    MILLY
If there's no body, how do you know he ain't?

                    EMMA
She got you there, Kate.

                    KATE
Oh...pish tosh!

                    MILLY
Pish tosh me all you want, somethin' happened to him out
there in the glen last night and it wasn't somethin' pretty.

                    EMMA
All they found was a pumpkin.

                    MILLY
A smashed pumpkin.

                    KATE
You're a smashed pumpkin.

                    EMMA
And his hat.

                    MILLY
There you go! Murdered!

                    KATE
Murdered, my foot! All you got is a dead hat!

                    MILLY
Brom and Carlotta and that crowd! They know somethin' about
this! There's a story, there, I'll tell you that!

                    EMMA
Well, tell _me_! How did it all start?

                    KATE
Oooh...if you must know...it all began three months ago when
he showed up. Mr. Crane. The first ones he run into were the
wastrels at the Sleepy Hollow tavern...

EMMA

What's a wastrel?

MILLY

Oh...you're so young....

Scene 2

Outside the Sleepy Hollow tavern. A few benches and tables, maybe a wooden barrel, some crates, with the tavern in the rear, a sign above its door.

JEB, WEED and SUSANNAH, three saloon ne'er-do-wells, hang about, pontificating in their ale. (Susannah is something of a tomboy.) Also loitering about are five Giddy Girls-- SALLY, JESSIE, MADDIE, LIZZIE and HANNAH, and some school children-- FELICITY, GEORGE, DOROTHY, LENORA and BENJAMIN.

As the LIGHTS COME UP, there is a huge laugh from everybody.

JEB

And that, my friends, is how Brom Bones took a cow from the Benson Farm, and switched it with a cow from the Smithers Farm, and nobody knew the difference.

Another big laugh.

SALLY

Oh, Jebediah Winthrop, that is a lie and you know it!

WEED

It ain't no lie, Sally.

SUSANNAH

My boy, Jeb, here don't know how to lie!

JEB

And that's the truth!

JESSIE

Oh, Susannah, you always take the side of the boys!

MADDIE

Yeah, you'd think you were a boy!

JEB
(to Susannah)
You mean you're not a boy?

SUSANNAH
(to Lizzie)
Do I look like a boy to you?

                    LIZZIE
Well...

                    HANNAH
You look more like a boy than Weed does!

                    All laugh.

                    WEED
That ain't funny!

                    SALLY
Weed...how did you ever get a name like that? Weed.

                    JEB
I got the answer to that...

                    WEED
              (to Jeb)
You be quiet!

                    JESSIE
Another lie comin' up!

                    JEB
His real name is Artemis.

                    MADDIE
Artemis???

                    LIZZIE
No wonder he goes with Weed.

                    JEB
And it so happened that one day his dear old mother was out
workin' in the garden, just as Brom Bones was makin' a
delivery from his butcher shop...

                    WEED
I told you not to...

                    JEB
And Weed comes into the kitchen, hungry as a horse, and spies
a beautiful green salad sittin' on the counter...

                    WEED
I didn't get no breakfast that day...

                    JEB
So he digs his hand into the "salad" and in three bites...

                    WEED
Four...

                              JEB
He gobbles up every blessed bit of it! And just as he shoves
the last handful into his kisser, his dear old mother comes
in the door with Brom and says, "Oh, Artemis! You just ate a
whole bowl of weeds!"

                    All laugh.

                              WEED
                         (embarrassed)
I left a couple of bites...

                              JEB
And when Brom saw what Artemis did, he started callin' him
"Weed" and it stuck!

                         Another huge laugh from everybody. Even
                         Weed joins in.

                              SUSANNAH
                         (raising her glass)
Three cheers for Brom Bones! Hip Hip...
                         (all "Hooray)
Hip Hip...
                         (again)
Hip Hip...

                         Again, they cheer, and as they do,
                         HENRY, the saloon keeper, enters.

                              HENRY
Good Lord in Heaven, do you all have to make so much fuss out
here?

                              SALLY
Oh, you love it, Henry. It makes it look like you actually
have customers!

                              HENRY
Customers, I wouldn't mind. Would it kill you all to come
inside and buy something to drink every now and again?

                              JEB
What? And spoil our virtuous reputations?

                         From inside the tavern we hear the
                         grating voice of Henry's wife, BESSIE.

                              BESSIE
                    (off)
HEN-RY!

                              HENRY
Oh, dear Lord...

                         BESSIE
                       (appears)
Henry! I just had a conversation with all them dirty glasses
on the counter in there...

                         HENRY
I know, dear, I...

                         BESSIE
I says to them, "Glasses, you are very dirty. Are you goin'
to clean yourselves up?"

                         HENRY
Bessie...

                         BESSIE
And you know what them dirty glasses said to me, Henry?

                         HENRY
I can't...imagine...

                         BESSIE
They said nothin'. You wanna know why, Henry?

                         HENRY
I just...

                         BESSIE
Because they're GLASSES!

                         HENRY
I'm sorry, dear...

                         BESSIE
Get inside and get to work!

                    She stalks off.

                         SUSANNAH
There's a sweet, quiet room waitin' for you in Heaven,
Henry...

                         HENRY
Can't come soon enough.
                    (shrugs, and looks down the
                     road)
Any sign of that new Schoolmaster?

                         SALLY
There's a new Schoolmaster?

                         HENRY
Well, of course there is! You knew Carlotta Van Derp ran the
last one out of the county.

                         JEB
For good and permanent?

                         HENRY
For good and permanent. His lifestyle was a little
too...frivolous for Miss Van Derp.

                         JESSIE
Everybody's a little too frivolous for Miss Van Derp.

                         HENRY
Well, he should be here presently. The coach is past due.
Send him in to me when he gets here.
               (sees something down the road)
Oh, no...

                              He tries to make it back inside, but
                              fails.

                              HARRIET and GERTRUDE, a couple of
                              village matrons, appear, and catch him.

                         HARRIET
Henry! We'd like to speak to you!

                         HENRY
Just a minute, ladies!
               (under breath, to others)
Now see what you done?
               (steps over to the matrons)
What can I do for you, this fine day?

                         GERTRUDE
It was fine, until...
               (points disapprovingly at the
               tavern folks)

                         HARRIET
I thought we agreed at the last church council meeting that
it would be preferable for you to keep these...customers
inside your establishment.

                         GERTRUDE
I can smell their breaths all the way from my back porch.

                              The wastrels attempt to breathe heavily
                              in their direction, to the stifled
                              delight of the Giddy Girls.

                         GERTRUDE (cont'd)
STOP BREATHING, YOU PEOPLE!
               (instantly, they do, holding
               their breath)
That's better.
               (they breathe out, in unison)

                         HENRY
I've tried, ladies, I've tried. But it is a public road, you
know.

                         HARRIET
Well...if that is your attitude, I see no alternative but to
report this to Carlotta Van Derp!

                         HENRY
Oh, please, don't do that...

                         GERTRUDE
We'll see what she says about these...ruffians. Come,
Harriet!

                         *And they strut away. Jeb starts a chant
                         as Henry walks back to the group...*

                         JEB
Henry got in trouble...Henry got in trouble...Henry got in
trouble...

                         *All join in until Henry reaches his
                         doorway and screams.*

                         HENRY
ALL RIGHT!
          (they all stop)
Someday...someday you're all going to push me just...a
little...too far. And when you do...

                         *BROM BONES and EZEKIEL enter. Brom is
                         brawny, bold and bombastic. Ezekiel
                         is...well, something of a weasel.*

                         BROM
And when they do, Henry, I'll be there to push you right over
the edge!

                         *As Henry moves quickly and disgustedly
                         into the tavern, all greet Brom
                         cordially, shouting out "Brom!" Ezekiel
                         steps in front of Brom and shoves some
                         people off a bench to make room.*

                         EZEKIEL
All right! All right! That's enough! Give us some room here!
          (room has been made)
There you go, Brom! I made room for you on the bench!

                         BROM
          (sitting amidst the throng)
Yes, you did, Ezekiel. Thank you. Your obviousness is matched
only by your obsequiousness!

                         EZEKIEL
          (thinks this is a compliment)
Why, thank you.

                         The Giddy Girls surround Brom.

> SALLY

Oh, Brom, where did you learn all those big, big words!

> BROM

Books, my dear Sally! Books!

> MADDIE

So many syllables!

> LIZZIE

Say another big word, Brom...please!

> BROM

Well...

> HANNAH

Oh, yes, Brom...say another big word for us...Please...

> > *The Giddy Girls go into a chorus of*
> > *"Please...Please...Please..."*

> BROM

Oh, all right. Let me think...

> EZEKIEL

Quiet, everybody! Brom is gonna say a big word!
> (beat)
Go ahead, Brom.

> > *Brom thinks as the Girls lean in.*

> BROM

I've got one...
> > (the Girls gast; he clears his
> > throat)
PERSPICACITY!

> > *The Girls swoon.*

> SALLY

Oh, Brom...tell us what it means!

> BROM
> (beat, retaining bombast)
I don't know. I heard it once in a sermon at a funeral and I
fell in love with it. It just sounds so...beautiful coming
from my lips. Don't you agree?

> > *All the Girls swoon and giggle and*
> > *agree.*

> SUSANNAH
> (moving in)
All right, enough of this girliness. What kind of mischief
are we up to today, Brom?

> JEB

Yes! We haven't done a good prank in almost a week!

                         BROM
Has it been that long?

                         WEED
Eight days!

                         JEB
That's almost a week...

                         BROM
Well, then, we must come up with something really, really
devilish...

                         The Girls swoon again. Ezekiel tries to
                         organize them...

                         EZEKIEL
All right! Give him room! Brom needs room to think!

                         As they do give him room, ICHABOD CRANE
                         appears, satchel in hand. He is an
                         awkward looking fellow, with a bookish
                         air about him. He takes off his cap and
                         greets the folks.

                         ICHABOD
Excuse me?

                         BROM
Why? What did you do?

                         Brom waits. Nobody laughs. He looks to
                         Ezekiel, and prompts him to inform the
                         citizenry that humor has been achieved.
                         He does.

                         EZEKIEL
That was a joke! Come on! Ha! Ha! Ha! Ha!

                         They then laugh..

                         ICHABOD
Ah! Yes! Humor! The lifesblood of existence!

                         BROM
                    (approaches Ichabod)
Where are you heading, friend?

                         ICHABOD
I believe I'm heading here. Is this the village of Sleepy
Hollow?

                         BROM
It's the village of Tarrytown. This little nook in the
village is called Sleepy Hollow. And who might you be?

                              ICHABOD
I might be...the new Schoolmaster!
                    (catches himself)
Oh! I made my own joke!

                              Eveerybody starts to laugh. Ezekiel
                              cuts them off instantly.

                              ICHABOD (cont'd)
                    (looks, see a pail)
Oh, is that water! I wonder if I might...

                              BROM
Of course! Drink up, friend!

                              Ichabod moves to the pail to get a
                              drink. Weed steps to Brom.

                              WEED
Henry said to let him know when the Schoolmaster arrived.
I'll go in and tell him...
                    (starts to tavern)

                              BROM
                    (stopping Weed)
Not...so fast, little Weed...

                              WEED
But...

                              BROM
Not so fast...let's see where this...encounter brings us
first, shall we?

                              JEB
Yes! Let's see!

                              Ichabod has finished. Steps back to the
                              group. He removes a slip of paper from
                              his pocket.

                              ICHABOD
If you would kindly direct me to the Van Fenster Farm...that
is where I am to lodge for the week.

                              BROM
The Van Fenster Farm, you say?

                              ICHABOD
Yes. I stay there the first week, and then, in subsequent
weeks, I will lodge with the various families of my various
students. It is part of my agreement with Miss Van Derp.

                              BROM
Well, I'd be happy to direct you to the Van Fenster Farm.
Here's what you do...

> *As he dispenses these directions, the folks listening in have to stifle back giggles, because they know Brom is sending Ichabod on a wild goose chase.*

                    BROM (cont'd)
                 (points as he directs)
Now...you see that road right there?

                    ICHABOD
I do!

                    BROM
That long, long road that turns at the pine tree and leads to that red barn in the distance there?

                    ICHABOD
Yes!

                    BROM
You see that road?

                    ICHABOD
Yes!

                    BROM
Don't take that road!

                    ICHABOD
No?

                    BROM
No.

                    ICHABOD
But it looks like the...only road to take.

                    BROM
You'd think so. But we know better. Don't we friends?

> *Everybody agrees vocally.*

                    BROM (cont'd)
No, what you want to do is go through that cornfield there, you see? And when you get to the other side of the cornfield-- it will take you some time, but don't give up, keep on plowing through the cornfield--when you get to the other side, you'll come upon a steep, steep hill.

                    ICHABOD
I will?

                    BROM
You will. And what you do when you get to that steep, steep hill, is, you climb it.

                    ICHABOD
I do.

                    BROM
All the way to the top.

                    ICHABOD
All the way.

                    BROM
All the way! And when you get to the top...

                    ICHABOD
The top.

                    BROM
The tippity top...you go down the hill.

                    ICHABOD
Down.

                    BROM
All the way down. To the bottom. And when you get to the
bottom...you'll come upon a stream.

                    ICHABOD
Oh, dear...

                    BROM
And a rowboat.

                    ICHABOD
Oh, dear.

                    BROM
Get in the rowboat.

                    ICHABOD
Oh, dear.

                    BROM
And row to the other side of the stream.

                    ICHABOD
Row.

                    EZEKIEL
Row!

                    BROM
Row. Your boat. Gently down the stream. And on the other side
of that stream, you will find the Van Fenster Farm.

                         *By this time, the folks listening are
                         about to bust a gut.*

                    ICHABOD
It seems like a...labyrinthine journey.

                    SALLY
Hey! He knows big words too!

                         BROM
Not at all! Shouldn't take you more than a few hours.

                         ICHABOD
Oh, dear...

                         BROM
But you'd better be on your way! Sun'll be down soon!

                         ICHABOD
Then I must hurry! Thank you for your assistance...Mr...?

                         BROM
Van Brunt! Abraham Van Brunt. But all my friends call me
Brom. Brom Bones! Isn't that right, friends!

                    They all shout "Brom!"

                         ICHABOD
Well, then, far be it from me, Brom, to eschew your
friendship!

                         WEED
Eschew?

                         JEB
Bless you.

                         ICHABOD
Thank you...Brom! Thank you all!

                    Ichabod picks up his satchel and heads
                    off. As he does, the throng offers
                    various calls of "Goodbye" "Good
                    luck..." etc...

                    And when they are sure he's out of
                    earshot, they burst into almost violent
                    gales of laughter.

                         JEB
Oh, Brom, that's one of your best ever!

                         WEED
Through the cornfield...!

                         SUSANNAH
All the way up the hill...all the way down the hill...!

                         JEB
And then he gets into the rowboat...!

                         SUSANNAH
With the hole in it!

                         WEED
He'll never make it to the other side!

Everybody is still laughing.

                    BROM
But if he does...if he does...where will he be?

                    SALLY
The Van Fenster farm!

                    BROM
So I wasn't lyin'!

                    Another mammoth roar of laughter as
                    Henry comes back out.

                    HENRY
Will you all please control yourselves!
          (they calm down a bit)
What is going on here?

                    BENJAMIN
          (one of the school children, a
          goody-two-shoes)
Brom just sent the Schoolmaster to the Van Fenster farm!

                    HENRY
What!

                    MADDIE
Through the cornfield!

                    HENRY
The cornfield!

                    JESSIE
In the rowboat!

                    HENRY
The rowboat!
          (to Jeb)
I told you to send him in to me!

                    JEB
Oops.

                    HENRY
Oops! Is that all you can say? Oops!
          (to Weed)
What about you?

                    WEED
          (nudged on by Jeb)
Oops.

                    Big laugh from everybody.

                    BENJAMIN
We have to help him!

                    HENRY
                (flustered)
Yes, we do, Benjamin...take the road and run over to the Van
Fenster farm, and meet him there. Then bring him back here.

                    BENJAMIN
Yes, sir!
                (he starts to run off)

                    HENRY
Wait!
                (he grabs a towel off the
                 table)
Better take this.

                    BENJAMIN
                (grabs towel)
Yes, sir!

                        Benjamin starts off again, but stops
                        and moves to stand directly in front of
                        the towering Brom.

                    BENJAMIN (cont'd)
                (to Brom)
Why don't you pick on somebody your own size!

                    BROM
Like who?

                    BENJAMIN
Like me!

                        Benjamin raises his fist to Brom, but
                        Henry stops him.

                    HENRY
Benjamin! Go!

                    BENJAMIN
                (disgusted)
Ah...
                (he runs off)

                    BESSIE
                (off)
HEN-RY!

                    HENRY
Oh, good Lord again...

                    BESSIE
                (appears)
Guess what, Henry?

                    HENRY
What, dear?

                         BESSIE
I just had another talk with them dirty glasses...

                              HENRY
I'll be right...

                              BESSIE
Know what they said this time?

                              HENRY
Bessie...

                              BESSIE
Still nothin'. Know why?

                              HENRY
I...

                              BESSIE
Because they're STILL GLASSES. And they're STILL DIRTY!

                              HENRY
I'm sorry, I...

                              BESSIE
                    (gently)
Henry...

                              HENRY
Yes?

                              BESSIE
Love of my life...

                              HENRY
Yes, dear...

                              BESSIE
GET TO WORK!

                         She stalks back inside.

                         *Henry heads for the tavern door, and
                         looks back to Brom.*

                              HENRY
Brom Bones...one of these days your pranks are going to get
you in deep, deep trouble.

                         *Brom rises, and looking very sincere
                         and penitent, walks over to Henry, and
                         puts his arm around his shoulders.*

                              BROM
Henry...from the bottom of my heart, all I can say is...I'm
sorry.

                         HENRY
                     (taken aback)
         Well...that's a start, I guess.

                         BROM
         I'm sorry...I wasn't over there to see him sink in that boat!

                                   *Another mammoth laugh from everybody as
                                   the LIGHTS CHANGE back to the
                                   Gossipers.*

                         MILLY
         Anyway, that's what we heard.

                         EMMA
         I know those people are rowdy, but...

                         KATE
         Rowdy! That's a polite word for it!

                         MILLY
         They're criminals is what they are! And there's no bigger
         criminal than Brom Bones!

                         KATE
         But he gets away with it!

                         MILLY
         Indeed, he does!

                         KATE
         And we know why he does!

                         MILLY
         Indeed, we do!

                         EMMA
         You do?

                         KATE
         We do! And so do you!

                         EMMA
         I do?

                         MILLY
         You do. So tell us. Tell me and tell Kate. Why do you think
         Brom Bones gets away with what he does?

                         EMMA
         Uh....

                         KATE
         You know.

                         EMMA
         I do?

                              KATE
You do.

                              MILLY
You do! So...go on...tell us...tell us...

                              KATE
TELL US!

                              MILLY
TELL US WHY BROM BONES GETS AWAY WITH WHAT HE DOES!

                              EMMA
                   (quietly)
He's cute?

                         MILLY & KATE
HE'S CUTE!

                              KATE
That's exactly it!

                              MILLY
And you can't tell me him and his rowdy people had nothin' to
do with...whatever happened to Mr. Crane!

                              EMMA
But...murder?

                              KATE
                   (to Milly)
Oh, don't be silly...

                              MILLY
MURDER! Is what I'm sayin'.

                              EMMA
Not tha Ghost?

                              MILLY
Not the Ghost! Murder by a human person, is what I'm sayin'.
Murder!

                              EMMA
Well, what about Miss Van Derp? How is she mixed up with Brom
Bones?

                              MILLY
                   (beat, to Kate)
Tell 'er.

                              KATE
I'm not tellin' her. You tell 'er.

                              MILLY
I'm not tellin' her.

                    KATE
Well, I'm not tellin' her.

                    MILLY
All right, I'll tell her.

                    EMMA
Good!

                    MILLY
Well, you know who Carlotta Van Derp is...

                    EMMA
Oh, yes. I'm afraid of her.

                    KATE
There's ain't a soul in Tarrytown who's not afraid of her.

                    MILLY
I thought I was tellin' this. Are you gonna tell?

                    KATE
I'm not gonna tell.

                    MILLY
Then be quiet while I tell...
            (beat)
Well, from what I heard, the day after Mr. Crane arrived,
Carlotta rounded up another couple of witches...

                    KATE
            (reprimanding)
Milly!

                    MILLY
Friends. Rounded up a couple of friends, and they plotted out
how they wanted the new Schoolmaster to behave himself...

                    *LIGHTS CHANGE to Carlotta's home. She
                    is well-to-do, but we don't need much
                    setting embellishment. A chair or two,
                    and a table will suffice.*

                    *CARLOTTA Van Derp appears. She is a
                    spinster-ish, cackling harpy adorned in
                    black. She calls out to her maid,
                    ABIGAIL, who is frightened of her own
                    shadow, which makes working for
                    Carlotta a hideous ordeal.*

                    CARLOTTA
            (quietly)
Abigail...
            (no response, a little louder)
Abigail...
            (again, nothing; she hollers)
ABIGAIL!!!!

Abigail enters. Her only defense is to
talk fast and do Carolotta's bidding.

ABIGAIL

Yes, Miss Carlotta! Yes! Yes! You wailed! I'm here! Yes! Yes!
How can I help? How can I be of assistance? What can I do to
do your bidding? You know that's why I'm here. You know that
I always will do each and every...

CARLOTTA

Well, the first thing you can do is stop talking.

ABIGAIL

I can do that. Yes. Yes, I can..I can do that. I can
definitely and absolutely do that very thing. I can...
(gets it)
Oh.
(finally stops talking, bows
her head)

CARLOTTA

I have been informed that the new Schoolmaster has arrived in
the village. Am I correct?

ABIGAIL

Well, of course you're correct, Miss. I can't think of
another time since I've been your maid, Miss, that you
haven't been correct. In fact, I would be willing to place a
wager that in your entire life, correctness has been
something that you have always excelled in, because of all
the people in the world I've known who have been correct,
nobody in my experience has ever been more...

CARLOTTA

STOP!
(beat)
Stop.

ABIGAIL

Yes'm.

CARLOTTA

And has the new Schoolmaster appeared at the school?

ABIGAIL

Well, you know, I can't say, really, Miss, because,
well...you know...I've only walked by the school on my way to
the market, you know, and while it seems there is a gentleman
there with the children who I haven't seen before, I can't
rightly say that he's the Schoolmaster, because, you know, I
haven't heard him or seen him actually mastering the children
at the school because I couldn't see the children bein'
mastered through the windows, only him, and for all I know,
he coulda been masterin' or not masterin'...

CARLOTTA

YES OR NO!

ABIGAIL
YES! YES!

CARLOTTA
It is my understanding from his letter of application that he
is an unattached gentleman.

ABIGAIL
Well, I didn't see anybody attached to him when I saw him
through the window.

CARLOTTA
(beat)
Do you have any idea, Abigail, how difficult it is to
communicate with you?

ABIGAIL
I imagine it must be a challenge, Miss.

CARLOTTA
I want you to do something for me...

ABIGAIL
I can do that. I can definitely do that. Just tell me what it
is you...

CARLOTTA
(growing in intensity as she
speaks)
I want you to visit this new Schoolmaster and remind him
that, per our agreement, I will not tolerate any of the
tomfoolery that the previous unattached Schoolmaster
perpetrated on the young women of our village. I will not
abide such a hedonistic and frivolous waste of time and
energy! He is to instruct the children in arithmetic,
spelling and history, then go home at the end of the day and
sit by his fire reading the bible until he falls asleep. That
will be the extent of his...activity...while he is pedagogue
of Sleepy Hollow. Tell him that I, Carlotta Van Derp, have
lived in Sleepy Hollow longer than any other human being and
what I say must be taken very, very...very seriously. If he
strays from the above noted tasks as Schoolmaster, he will
suffer the consequences, which will be severe, painful and
painfully intractable! Do you understand me, Abigail?

ABIGAIL
(beat)
Not even close.

CARLOTTA
Oh, never mind! Get out of my sight! Go...sweep the belfry!

ABIGAIL
Yes'm!
(starts off)
What's the belfry!

CARLOTTA
Just follow the bats! Out!

> Abigail races away. As she does,
> Harriet and Gertrude, enter and bump
> into her.

HARRIET
Watch where you're going, wretch!

GERTRUDE
Be careful, you clumsy ox!

> Abigail freezes, looks at all of them.

ABIGAIL
(carefully)
Hello?

> At once, they all shout "OUT!" Abigail
> screams and leaves.

CARLOTTA
Oh, she is so clumsy and awkward! A complete and utter waste
of earthly oxygen! I do apologize, ladies.

HARRIET
Why do you keep her on?

GERTRUDE
If she's as useless as you say, why not just let her go?

CARLOTTA
I enjoy watching her cringe in fright. You understand.

HARRIET
Of course.

GERTRUDE
Absolutely.

CARLOTTA
I assume you want something from me?

HARRIET
Oh, yes! Very important!

CARLOTTA
(not thrilled)
What is it?

GERTRUDE
You must do something about the tavern.

CARLOTTA
And what is it I must do?

                         HARRIET
You must...rid it of its disgusting clientele!

                         CARLOTTA
I see.

                         GERTRUDE
They loiter about, day in and day out...

                         HARRIET
Accomplishing nothing...

                         GERTRUDE
And giving the village a bad name!

                         CARLOTTA
Well...I assure you, ladies, that I will see to it that the
tavern is closed forever!

                         HARRIET
Good!

                         GERTRUDE
Perfect!

                         HARRIET
It's about time!

                         CARLOTTA
You'll no doubt benefit fro the time your husbands will now
be able to spend at home with you in the evening.

                         HARRIET
Oh?

                         GERTRUDE
Oh?

                         CARLOTTA
Every...evening...sitting there...staring at you...puttering
around the kitchen...moving your furniture here and there to
keep from being bored...talking...incessantly...to
you...talking...because now they have no place to...

                         HARRIET
Oh, please don't close the tavern!

                         GERTRUDE
Please!

                         CARLOTTA
Whatever you say.

                         GERTRUDE
Thank heavens!

                         Carlotta reaches for her wrap and
                         bonnet.

                         CARLOTTA
Now...come with me...we must visit the new Schoolmaster.

                         HARRIET
                       (excitedly)
Oh? Has he misbehaved already?

                         CARLOTTA
That's what I want to find out!

                         GERTRUDE
Oh, goody! I do hope he has! I love it when you put people in
their place!

                         CARLOTTA
It's a thankless job...everybody hates and fears me...I live
a lonely, wretched life devoid of joy and happiness, and in
turn I make everbody else's life miserable.
                       (beat)
I love it so!

                    They all cackle and leave.

                    LIGHTS CHANGE back to the Gossipers.

                         EMMA
But you didn't tell me how Miss Carlotta was mixed up with
Brom Bones!

                         KATE
How are you feelin'?

                         EMMA
Uh...fine...

                         MILLY
No headache?

                         EMMA
No.

                         KATE
No sniffles? No congestion?

                         EMMA
No.

                         MILLY
Think you're gonna be with us a while?

                         KATE
Won't be headin' to your deathbed any time soon?

                         EMMA
Goodness, no!

                         KATE
Then what's your hurry?

                    MILLY
We'll tell the story in our own good time. It ain't all that
simple, you know.

                    KATE
Not when it comes down to...what it came down to between Mr.
Crane and Brom.

                    EMMA
What...did it come down to?

                    KATE
          (beat; then to Milly)
You tell her.

                    MILLY
I'm not tellin' her. You tell her.

                    KATE
I'm not tellin' her!

                    EMMA
Tell me what!

                    MILLY
You can tie me to a tree trunk, pull my hair out by the roots
and put needles in my eyeballs, I ain't tellin' her!

                    EMMA
PLEASE!!!

                    MILLY
All right, I'll tell her.

                    EMMA
What did it come down to between Mr. Crane and Brom?

                    MILLY & KATE
Sex!

                    MILLY
I thought I was tellin' her!

                    KATE
Well, it jumped out of me. I couldn't help it.

                    MILLY
Sex jumped out of you?

                    KATE
It happens.

                    EMMA
Tell me!!!!

                    MILLY
All right...but in order to tell it correct...we have to tell
you about Mr. Crane and his schoolroom...

LIGHTS CHANGE to the school room, which is simply a couple of benches and a rostrum for Ichabod.

All the students, except Benjamin, are running wild, playing tag, making a lot of noise. After a few moments, Benjamin stands and shouts.

BENJAMIN
All right! QUIET DOWN! QUIET DOWN!!!!
(everybody stops)
Take your seats.
(they do; Benjamin calls off)
They're ready for you, Schoolmaster!

The students, under their breath, mimick Benjamin's "They're ready for you, Schoolmaster," as Ichabod enters with his book bag and stick, and takes his place at the rostrum. He sniffs the air.

ICHABOD
Ah, the pungeant aroma of perspiring children! The perfect olfactory ambiance of the schoolroom!

BENJAMIN
They were playing tag, Mr Crane. I put a stop to it!

ICHABOD
As well you should, Benjamin! There's a time for play, and a time for study. Since Benjamin has put an end to playtime, let us all open our history books to chapter three, entitled, "Salem," and read silently.
(they begin to do this)
Uh...Felicity...would you step to the rostrum for a moment?

FELICITY
Step to the where?

ICHABOD
Just come here, child. Come here.

FELICITY
(approaches)
Yes, Mr. Crane?

ICHABOD
Felicity, according to my calendar, I am scheduled to have dinner at your lovely home on Sunday, is that correct?

FELICITY
If you say so.

                         ICHABOD
I do say so. As you may or may not know, my agreement with
this lovely village as your Schoolmaster is that all my
victuals will be consumed at the abodes of the families of my
students.

                         FELICITY
I know a few of those words, sir.

                         ICHABOD
Tell me, Felicity...is your mother a good cook?

                         DOROTHY
                    (raises hand)
Schoolmaster?

                         ICHABOD
                    (still with Felicity)
I mean, when she prepares a meal, does she....

                         DOROTHY
Schoolmaster! Schoolmaster!

                         ICHABOD
Yes, what is it, Dorothy?

                         DOROTHY
                    (reads)
It says here...in this book...that there were witches in
Salem!

                         ICHABOD
Well, I don't know if...just...keep reading...
                    (to Felicity)
Felicity, about your mother's pies...

                         LENORA
                    (also reading)
And that they "cast evil spells on the citizens!"

                         ICHABOD
Lenora, I don't think...

                         BENJAMIN
There's no such thing as witches!

                         GEORGE
                    (also in book)
And when they got found out, they were hung by their necks
until they were dead!
                    (makes hanging gesture and
                     vocal)

                         DOROTHY
Dead?

                         LENORA
Dead?

                         GEORGE
Dead.
                  (makes hanging gesture and
                  vocal again)

                         Ichabod says nothing. He looks at
                         Felicity.

                         FELICITY
Boisenberry.

                         ICHABOD
What?

                         FELICITY
My mother's pies. They're usually boisenberry.

                         At this point, Lenora throws her book
                         on the floor.

                         LENORA
Witches!

                         DOROTHY
Black magic!

                         GEORGE
                  (makes hanging gesture and
                  vocal again)
                         BENJAMIN
No! Such! Thing!

                         FELICITY
Can I go back to my bench now, Schoolmaster?

                         ICHABOD
Uh...yes, Felicity. Yes. Boisenberry, you say?

                         FELICITY
Yes.

                         ICHABOD
Good. Good. Take your seat, please.

                         She does. The students stare at him.

                         LENORA
Tell us about the witches, Schoolmaster...

                         BENJAMIN
I told you, there's no such thing as...

                         ICHABOD
Oh...I wouldn't go so far as to say that, Benjamin.

*As Ichabod continues, he becomes more
and more uncomfortable discussing this
topic.*

BENJAMIN
Schoolmaster...you don't mean to say...

ICHABOD
The town where I was previously employed...Beverly,
Massachusetts...is only a stone's throw from Salem. And
during my time there, I was told a sufficient number of
stories...about witches and...ghostly figures of the
night...to convince me that...disbelief in
such...creatures...was a path better left untaken.

*He starts to roam around the room,
uneasily.*

FELICITY
You mean, you believe in spooks, Schoolmaster?

GEORGE
And witches...?

DOROTHY
And goblins...?

LENORA
And spirits...?

FELICITY
And...the devil!

ICHABOD
(sufficiently frightened)
Oh, please, children...enough!
(changing the subject)
Take out your arithmetic books!

*The students now begin to surround him
and nudge him toward the wall. Dorothy
sneaks over to the wall.*

DOROTHY
(beginning to taunt)
I think the Schoolmaster...is afraid of ghosts!

GEORGE
And creatures that creep around in the night!

LENORA
Creepy creatures!

FELICITY
Are you afraid, Schoolmaster!

*As they hem him in, they all begin to
make spooky noises.*

                        BENJAMIN
He is not afraid! Are you, Schoolmaster?

                        ICHABOD
                    (losing it)
Well, I....I mean to say, I...I don't...

                        At this point, he is almost to the
                        wall, facing away from Dorothy, who
                        says...

                        DOROTHY
BOO!

                        Ichabod screams and goes to hide behind
                        his rostrum, as the students (except
                        Benjamin) laugh uproariously. Benjamin
                        grabs the big school bell, and begins
                        to ring it.

                        BENJAMIN
That's enough! School is out for the day! Everybody go home!

                        FELICITY
But it isn't even noontime...

                        BENJAMIN
OUT!!! ALL OF YOU!!! OUT!!!

                        The students grab their bags and books
                        and cheerfully exit. As they do,
                        Carlotta, Harriet and Gertrude enter,
                        running into the children as they tear
                        out the door.

                        CARLOTTA
What is the meaning of this?

                        HARRIET
It's not even time for the midday meal!

                        GERTRUDE
They're running away like thieves!

                        CARLOTTA
Schoolmaster!

                        Benjamin has gathered up the withering
                        Ichabod and brought him to his feet. As
                        she brushes him off, she fashions an
                        explanation for the ladies.

                        BENJAMIN
Uh...the Schoolmaster was...demonstrating...the art
of...of...acting! Yes! He was...playing out for the students
the last scene from...from...

                    ICHABOD
              (catching on)
King Lear.

                    BENJAMIN
King Lear! Yes!

                    CARLOTTA
              (with great skepticism)
Is that so?

                    BENJAMIN
Yes! And he told the children to go home and act out the
scene for their mothers and fathers while it was fresh in
their minds!

                    CARLOTTA
              (to Harriet)
Do you believe him?

                    HARRIET
He's very convincing.

                    CARLOTTA
              (to Gertrude)
Do you believe him?

                    GERTRUDE
It's a plausible explanation.

                    CARLOTTA
              (to Benjamin)
I don't believe you for a second!

                    HARRIET
He lies!

                    GERTRUDE
Complete fabrication!

                    BENJAMIN
              (aside, to Ichabod)
I tried.

                    ICHABOD
See you tomorrow, Benjamin.

                    Benjamin grabs his things, and rushes
                    out.

                    CARLOTTA
What...in the name of all that is good and holy...are you up
to, Mr. Crane?

                    ICHABOD
Well, to be truthful, Miss Van Derp, I was...I was
demonstrating for the students--in a theatrical sense--the
dark history of Salem, Massachusetts.

                              CARLOTTA
By hiding behind your desk?

                              ICHABOD
Well, it is dark back there...

                              CARLOTTA
Mr. Crane, I believe I made it quite clear that I would
tolerate no frivolity from you as Village Schoolmaster.
                    (to Harriet and Gertrude)
Did I not make this quite clear?

                              HARRIET
Oh, you did, Carlotta.

                              GERTRUDE
Clear as a baby's teardrop.

                              CARLOTTA
                    (reacts to this, then plunges
                      on)
Schoolmaster?

                              ICHABOD
You did, Miss Van Derp. You did.

                              CARLOTTA
I condsider it my duty and responsibility to make certain
that our young people are educated in reading, writing and
arithmetic only! Not in...theatre! If that, in fact, is what
you were doing...

                              ICHABOD
Well, you see, I...

                              CARLOTTA
There is no place for theatre in the schoolroom!

                              HARRIET
No place!

                              GERTRUDE
Patooie!

                              CARLOTTA
                    (again, reacts to Gertrude)
This will be my only warning, Mr. Crane. Should I witness or
be advised of one more lapse in judgment on your part, I'll
see to it that you are dismissed immediately. Is THAT clear?

                              ICHABOD
Very clear, Miss Van Derp.

                              CARLOTTA
Ladies...
                    (she starts out, they follow,
                      she stops at door)

CARLOTTA (cont'd)

And...lest it be left unsaid...it is absolutely mandatory
that you remain unattached as long as you are in the employ
of this schoolhouse. If you want to...attach yourself to
somebody...seek employment elsewhere. You know what
unattached means, do you not, Mr. Crane?

GERTRUDE

No women!

HARRIET

None whatsoever!

GERTRUDE

Patooie!

Both Harriet and Carlotta react.

ICHABOD

I have long been...unmoved by the fairer sex, Miss Van Derp.
I can't imagine anyone who would change that. I am...and will
remain...unattached.

CARLOTTA

Of course you will. Because that's the way I want it.
                    (approaches him)
Do you know what you are Mr. Crane?

ICHABOD

I...uh...

CARLOTTA

You're a man. And that, I find...intolerable!
                    (to ladies)
Ladies...?

> *Carlotta leads the ladies out the door.
> Ichabod begins to tidy up the room, and
> the LIGHTS DIM and come up full on the
> Gossips. We remain in the same scene,
> however.*

MILLY

Now, from what I understand, Mr. Crane was very sincere when
he said he was...unmoved by the fairer sex.

KATE

Not surprising. I mean, look at him...he was afraid of his
own shadow.

MILLY

But it didn't take long for all that to change.

EMMA

How long?

KATE

About five minutes, as the rumor goes...

                              EMMA
Five minutes.

                              MILLY
Miss Van Derp was barely out the door when everything changed
for the Schoolmaster.

                              EMMA
But...what could possibly happen to change him in five
minutes?

                              MILLY
                         (to Kate)
You tell her.

                              KATE
I'm not tellin' her...

                              MILLY
Well, I'm not tellin' her...

                              KATE
Well, you're gonna have to because I'm not...

                              EMMA
WHAT HAPPENED???

                         MILLY & KATE
Katrina Van Tassel!

                         LIGHTS OUT on Gossips, UP FULL on the
                         schoolroom. Ichabod is finishing
                         tidying up. KATRINA Van Tassel enters.

                         KATRINA Van Tassel is an extremely
                         pretty, vivacious and wealthy young
                         woman. She is also uncompromisingly
                         flirtacious with all men, all the time.
                         Men will do anything for Katrina. All
                         men. All the time.

                              KATRINA
You must be Mr. Crane, the new Schoolmaster!

                              ICHABOD
                         (taken aback)
Oh...Oh...Indeed. Indeed, I am.

                              KATRINA
Permit me to introduce myself...

                              ICHABOD
Oh, my dear young lady, no need...no need! Why, there isn't a
male in the entire village...dare I say the entire
county...who doesn't know the charming, charming...ever so
charming...Katrina Van Tassel!

KATRINA

Why, Mr. Crane...you flatter me!

ICHABOD

I do?

KATRINA

You do.

ICHABOD

Well, good. Good! You must be flattered constantly. That
will be my only goal whenever I am in your presence.

KATRINA
(seemingly shy, but not really)

Oh, Mr. Crane...

ICHABOD

Please. Ichabod.

KATRINA

All right. Ichabod.
(thinking)
Ichabod...Would you mind if I called you...Icky?

ICHABOD

Icky?

KATRINA

Icky.

ICHABOD

Well...I mean...no one's ever called me Icky before. I
mean...as a name.

KATRINA

Oh, well, then, if you'd rather...

ICHABOD

No! NO! Please...please call me Icky. I will respond to that
name from you and only you from now on. To you, I am Icky.
Icky, Icky, Icky!

KATRINA

Icky!

ICHABOD

And I shall call you Katrina!

KATRINA
(seemingly taken aback)

Oh. Oh...I don't think...

ICHABOD

Oh...I'm so sorry. I mean...oh, dear.

KATRINA
You see...it's just...it's just...
(very flirtacious)
...so...so familiar.

ICHABOD
I...I...

KATRINA
(still flirting)
I mean, what would all the other boys think if they heard you
calling me Katrina...

ICHABOD
I...I...

KATRINA
They'd think...they'd think you and I...

ICHABOD
(hoping for the best)
Yes. Yes. You and I. Yes. What would they think?

KATRINA
They'd think...they'd think you and I were...sweethearts!

ICHABOD
(stammering)
Would they? Would they? I...I...I don't...I wouldn't want
to...

KATRINA
Of course, they might think the same thing if they heard me
calling you...Icky.

ICHABOD
(desperate)
Please...please...please...call me...Icky.

KATRINA
I'll think about it...
(steps away, coyly, turns back)
Icky.
(she leaves)

ICHABOD
(beat, to himself, totally
smitten)
She called me Icky!!!!

LIGHTS CHANGE to Gossips.

EMMA
But I thought Miss Katrina was promised to Brom Bones.

MILLY
Miss Katrina is promised to Miss Katrina.

                              KATE
The wiles of a cobra. That's what she has!

                              EMMA
Cobra? Isn't that a snake?

                              MILLY
Now you're catchin' on.

                              EMMA
But you still haven't explained to me how Miss Carlotta and
Brom Bones...

                              MILLY
Oh, your impatience is wearin' me thin!

                              KATE
And that would take a lot of impatience!

                              MILLY
Hush!

                              EMMA
It's so complicated.

                              MILLY
Keep followin' the story, Missy--you'll put the pudding
together.

                              KATE
"Put the pudding together?" What kind of phraseology is that?

                              MILLY
It just come to me. I'm very bright, you know.

                              KATE
I see. And you been keepin' that to yourself all these
years?

                              EMMA
Tell me!

                              MILLY
We already started tellin' you! We told you Carlotta had no
use for unattached men.

                              KATE
Attached or unattached, it makes no difference.

                              EMMA
Why was that?

                              KATE
Because when she was attached to one, he philandered on her.

                              EMMA
No!

                    MILLY
Yes!

                    KATE
So she threw him out, kept all his money, and she's hated men
ever since!

                    MILLY
Except for Brom Bones. She had a soft spot in her heart for
Brom Bones.

                    EMMA
Why?

                    KATE
Well, she didn't consider Brom to be a man.

                    EMMA
No?

                    MILLY
No. She considered him to be more like...like...

                    KATE
A tree.

                    MILLY
Yes. A tree.

                    KATE
Pleasant to look at, a little sappy, and completely harmless.

                    EMMA
Like a tree!s

                    KATE
You're a bright one, you are.

                    MILLY
But when little Miss Katrina set her sights on the
Schoolmaster...

                    KATE
That's when Carlotta went into high dudgeon!

                    MILLY
                (points to Kate)
Yes! I don't know what that means, but...Yes!

                    KATE
And it all came to a head outside the tavern, just one day
after Katrina's visit to the schoolroom...

                    LIGHTS CHANGE to outside the tavern.

*The Giddy Girls surround Brom and fawn
all over him as Ezekiel stands guard to
the side. The wastrels are also hanging
about, playing some kind of card game.*

                    SALLY
Oh, Brom, you look so handsome and virile today!

                    BROM
          (jokingly skeptical)
Just today?

                    JESSIE
I love the way the sun strikes your jaw!

                    BROM
          (Brom adjusts his jaw,
            impressing her even more)
Like this?

                    JESSIE
Ooh!

                    MADDIE
Lizzie...move over, you're shading the sun from Brom's jaw!

                    BROM
Watch that, Lizzie!

                    LIZZIE
Sorry, Brom!

                    DOROTHY
Which of us will you take for a walk tonight, Brom?

                    SALLY
It's my turn!

                    JESSIE
You went last night!

                    SALLY
But there was no moon! A walk is no good without a moon!

                    MADDIE
Who needs a moon when you walk with Brom!

                    LIZZIE
A walk with Brom needs no moon at all!

                    MADDIE
That's the same thing I said!

                    LIZZIE
I said it better!

                    DOROTHY
Oh, Brom, take me for a walk! I will be your moon!

> *At this point, all the Giddy Girls*
> *begin to vocally and physically fawn*
> *all over him in earnest, until he has*
> *to break it up.*

BROM

Girls, girls, girls!...Surely you have better things to do
than to fawn all over me!
(they giddily protest)
I mean...what am I but a simple country butcher, unworthy of
your affection.
(a bigger, louder protest from
the girls)

> *As they protest and slobber all over*
> *Brom, Katrina appears, twirling a*
> *parasol. Brom sees her, and wants to go*
> *to her, but he can't extract himself*
> *from the ladies. He signals to*
> *Ezekiel...*

BROM (cont'd)

Zeke! Zeke!

> *Ezekiel promptly moves in and shoves*
> *the girls away from Brom.*

EZEKIEL

All right! All right! That's enough adoration! Give Mr. Van
Brunt some breathing room, ladies! Let's go! Let's go!
(they are dispersed)
NOW JUST SIT THERE, AND KEEP YOUR BRITCHES WHERE THEY BELONG!
(to Brom)
There you go, Brom. I tamed 'em for you.

> *Ezekiel moves back to his guarding*
> *position as the Giddy Girls look on in*
> *disgust.*

> *Brom primps, and walks in Katrina's*
> *direction.*

BROM

Why, Katrina...I...didn't see you twirling there.

KATRINA
(still twirling her parasol)
Really, Brom? That surprises me. I was...twirling in your
direction.

BROM

Ah. Well, as you can see...I was...preoccupied.

KATRINA

Preoccupied?
(looks at girls)
Oh! I see! You were playing with your little friends!

                          SALLY
                 (starts to rush Katrina)
Hey!

                          EZEKIEL
                 (stops her)
Siddown!
                 (Sally sits, steaming)
Caught her in time, boss.

                          BROM
Thank you, Ezekiel.

                          KATRINA
                 (coyly)
Oh, Brom, I hope I haven't disrupted your afternoon
bacchanal.

                 Brom laughs.

                          JEB
What's a bacchanal?

                          SUSANNAH
Beats me.

                          WEED
Must be a card game. Should we play?

                          BROM
                 (disingenuously)
Well, if you must know, Katrina...I was...enjoying myself
with these ladies...

                 *He starts to move to the ladies. They
                 lean toward him in anticipation.
                 Ezekiel stops them.*

                          EZEKIEL
Uh uh. Lower your temperature. He's just toying with her.

                          KATRINA
                 (as he reaches the ladies,
                  again, very coyly)
Oh! I see! Well, then...I suppose I should just run along
and...

                          BROM
                 (turns back to her, as coyly as
                  she)
Of course, Katrina, if you were to...ask me nicely...

                 *At this point, Ichabod enters, along
                 with Benjamin. They both carry books.
                 Ichabod is preoccupied until he sees
                 Katrina. When he does, he drops all his
                 books. Benjmain begins to pick them up,
                 as Ichabod stutters...*

                              ICHABOD
It's K...K...K...K...K...

                              BENJAMIN
It's Miss Van Tassel.

                              ICHABOD
That's what I said.

                              KATRINA
                    (instantly switches gears)
Oh! Why, it's the Schoolmaster!

                         BROM
Huh? What?

                              KATRINA
                    (moving to Ichabod)
Icky! It's so very nice to see you! How are you today...
                    (in Brom's direction)
...Icky?

                         JEB
What did she call him?

                              SUSANNAH
Icky.

                         WEED
Icky?

                         JEB
Is that a name?

                              SUSANNAH
It's not a name. It's a condition.

                              KATRINA
Icky! Where are you headed this fine afternoon?

                              ICHABOD
Well, I....I....I....

                              BENJAMIN
We're going to the library.

                              KATRINA
The library!

                         JEB
I didn't know we had a library.

                              WEED
I didn't know we had books.

                              KATRINA
                    (all for Brom's benefit, of
                    course)

KATRINA (cont'd)
I haven't been to the library in ages! Would you mind if
I...tagged along?

BENJAMIN
Yes!

ICHABOD
Not at all!

KATRINA
Wonderful! It's such a lovely time for a walk!

> Katrina takes his arm and walks past
> Brom and everyone as they head out.
> Benjamin takes up the rear, holding all
> Ichabod's books, and his own. Ichabod
> stops a moment.

ICHABOD
Oh, by the way, Mr. Bones, I never did thank you for those
splendid directions to the Van Fenster farm. It was such a
stifling day! I thoroughly enjoyed my little dip in the
stream! Miss Van Tassel, shall we?

> He re-takes her arm, and they head off
> again. Just before the exit, Katrina
> looks back.

KATRINA
Oh...I almost forgot...you are all invited to my father's
farm for the Harvest Sociable next Friday night.

WEED
(jumps up)
Even me?

KATRINA
Even you, Artemis!

WEED
(sits down)
She called me Artemis!

KATRINA
It will be the most most wonderful evening! And my special
guest will be our new Schoolmaster, Mr. Ichabod Crane!
(starts off again, stops)
Brom, you should take a walk with one of these...charming
ladies. Just...
(really dismissing them)
...any one will do. 'Bye 'bye....

> Benjamin grunts, and they leave.

> Brom sits, flabbergasted. Nobody else
> speaks. Everybody waits for him to say
> something. He rises, looks down the
> road...

                              BROM
What. Just. Happened?

                              WEED
                    (steps over to Brom, speaks
                     with breathless abandon)
Oh, well, you see, you were sitting with the girls, here, and
they were hanging all over you, when Miss Katrina came by,
and you left the girls and went over to her and you started
fawning all over her. Then Miss Katrina started flirting with
you, and so you went back to the fawning ladies hoping to
make Miss Katrina jealous, but then the Schoolmaster came by
and dropped all his books, and Miss Katrina started flirting
with him. And then he told her he was going to the library,
so she said, Oh, that's nice, I think I'll go to the
library, too. And then she invited us all to the sociable
next Friday night. Even me. She called me Artemis! And then
Benjamin picked up the books and Miss Katrina took the
Schoolmaster's arm and they headed down the road to the
library, all the time you were sitting there in the middle of
the fawning ladies who stopped fawning because you were
flirting with Miss Van Tassel, and I think that's pretty much
what just happened.

                              BROM
                    (who has just been staring at
                     Weed)
Weed?

                              WEED
Yes, Brom.

                              BROM
Are you finished?

                              WEED
Uh...let's see...
                    (mumbles a recount of his
                     story)
You...ladies fawning...Miss Van Tassel...you fawning...her
flirting...you flirting...the Schoolmaster...calls me
Artemis...she's flirting again, this time with him...takes
the arm...Benjamin gets the books...off to the library...yep,
that's it. That's everything.

                              BROM
Good. Now...Weed...

                              WEED
Yes, Brom

                              BROM
                    (screams)
GET AWAY FROM ME!!!!!

                         Weed races back to his companions as
                         the Giddy Girls surround Brom.

                         SALLY
Oh, Brom, don't waste your time with her!

                         JESSIE
Everybody knows Katrina Van Tassel is just a snob.

                         MADDIE
I hate her!

                         LIZZIE
Everybody hates her!

                         JEB
                 (raises his hand)
I don't hate her!

                         SUSANNAH
                 (pulls his hand down)
You keep out of this!

                         WEED
She called me Artemis!

                         HANNAH
You can have any girl you want!

                         SALLY
Yes! Any girl! Any one of us! Any time you want!

                         MADDIE
Pick one!

                         JESSIE
Pick me!

                         MILLY
Me!

                         LIZZIE
Me!

                         HANNAH
Me!

                         They swarm him, repeating "Pick me!"
                         Finally, he steps away and stops them.

                         BROM
ALL RIGHT!
                 (they all freeze)
I pick...I pick...

                         He steps past them, and looks down the
                         road.

                         BROM (cont'd)
I pick...Katrina.

                          EZEKIEL
KATRINA! BOOM!

                          WEED
I knew he was gonna pick Katrina.

                          BROM
If that...Schoolmaster...thinks he's going to take my bride
to be away from me...he has another think coming! Ezekiel!

                          EZEKIEL
                    (goes to Brom)
Yes, Brom!

                          BROM
I want to be here, alone, when the Schoolmaster returns. Take
everyone inside and buy them a drink. On me!

                          EZEKIEL
Yes, Brom!
                    (he starts off)

                          BROM
Ezekiel!

                          EZEKIEL
                    (stops)
Yes, Brom!

                          BROM
Use your own money.

                          EZEKIEL
Yes, Brom!
                    (to all)
Everybody! Follow me inside! Drinks for everyone!

                              Everybody follows Ezekiel into the
                              tavern. Brom looks down the road.

                          BROM
Schoolmaster...I'm about to teach YOU a lesson...

                              LIGHTS DIM on Brom, UP FULL on
                              Gossipers.

                          EMMA
He was going to teach the Schoolmaster a lesson? Isn't
that...ironic?

                          MILLY
I don't know. Ask her. She's the one that reads.

                          KATE
Ironic, it was. But as it turned out, it wasn't the
Schoolmaster who learned the lesson.

                    EMMA
No?

                    MILLY
No.

                    KATE
Brom waited outside the tavern until the Schoolmaster and
Miss Katrina returned, and by the time they did, he had his
plan all figured out...

                    LIGHTS OUT on Gossipers, UP FULL
                    outside tavern.

                    Brom sits alone on a bench, as Benjamin
                    trudges in, carrying an even bigger
                    load of books. He trudges past Brom.

                    BROM
Benjamin...where's the Schoolmaster?

                    BENJAMIN
                    (with disgust, nodding to his
                     rear)
With the Queen of Sheba.

                    Benjamin grunts and leaves. Ichabod
                    enters with Katrina still on his arm.

                    KATRINA
                    (sees the brooding Brom, and
                     goes into action)
Oh, Mr. Crane...please recite that beautiful LOVE poem to me
again...

                    ICHABOD
Oh...you mean...the Shakespeare.

                    KATRINA
Yes....Yes....
                    (looks to Brom)
The Shakespeare.

                    ICHABOD
                    (clears throat; recites with
                     great, overly-dramatic
                     feeling)
Let me not to the marriage of true minds
Admit impediments. Love is not love
Which alters when it alteration finds
Or bends with the remover to remove:
O no! it is an ever-fixed mark
That looks on tempests and is never shaken;
It is the star to every wand'ring bark,
Whose worth's unknown, although his height be taken.
Love's not Time's fool, though rosy lips and cheeks
Within his bending sickle's compass come;
Love alters not with his brief hours and weeks,

                        ICHABOD (cont'd)
But bears it out even to the edge of doom:
If this be error and upon me proved,
I never writ, nor no man ever loved.

                        KATRINA
                    (fake swooning)
Oh! Did you hear that, Brom? He never writ, nor no man ever
loved!

                        ICHABOD
Well...I wasn't the one that never writ. It was Shakespeare.

                        KATRINA
Oh, Mr. Crane...thank you so much for the lovely, lovely
afternoon...

                        ICHABOD
Well...think nothing of it, Miss Katrina.

                        KATRINA
I must go home now. My father will be worried. I did so lose
track of the time...

                        ICHABOD
I could accompany you, if...

                        KATRINA
No! No...I need to be alone now, to...to...contemplate what
has happened to me today...

                        ICHABOD
Oh. Well...all right!

                        KATRINA
Goodbye. And thank you.
                    (starts off, stops)
Oh...I will see you at my home next Friday evening?

                        ICHABOD
Oh, absolutely...

                        BROM
                    (as Katrina starts off)
Katrina?

                        KATRINA
                    (stops)
Yes, Brom?

                        BROM
I'll be there as well.

                        KATRINA
Oh. You will?

                        BROM
Absolutely.

                    KATRINA
Oh. Well...I guess that's nice.
          (beat)
Goodbye...Icky!

                              She smiles and leaves Ichabod alone
                              with Brom. As they talk, Sally sneaks
                              out of the tavern and listens in the
                              shadows.

                    BROM
Pretty girl, isn't she?

                    ICHABOD
Oh...pretty isn't nearly a sufficient adjective for Miss
Katrina.

                    BROM
No?

                    ICHABOD
No. Beautiful! Ethereal! Exquisite! Magnificent!
Pulchritudinous! Radiant! Resplendent...

                    BROM
Rich!

                    ICHABOD
Re...what?

                    BROM
Rich. She's extremely rich.

                    ICHABOD
Oh. How extremely?

                    BROM
Extremely extremely. Whoever she chooses to marry is going to
find himself a very, very wealthy man.

                    ICHABOD
Well...isn't that...convenient.

                    BROM
It is indeed, especially since it seems you are at a decided
advantage over the rest of us poor souls when it comes to
winning the heart of Miss Van Tassel.

                    ICHABOD
          (enjoying this)
Hmm...it seems I am, aren't I?

                    BROM
Yes, and as your friend I should tell you that the one way to
assure yourself of winning that heart...

                    ICHABOD
And that dowry...

BROM
And that dowry...the one way to emerge victorious is to
impress her father.

ICHABOD
Oh. There's a father.

BROM
Baltus Van Tassel. The richest man in the Hudson Valley. Win
him over, and her hand, her heart...

ICHABOD
And her dowry...

BROM
And her dowry...will be yours.

ICHABOD
And...do you have any suggestions as to how I might do this?

BROM
Well...I was saving this little tidbit of informaton to use
myself, but since it looks like I'm out of the running, I'll
gladly pass it along to you.

ICHABOD
You're such a good man.

BROM
When you meet him...when you meet Baltus Van Tassel at the
sociable next Friday night, you must insist that he shakes
your hand.

                    In the shadows, we see Sally reacting
                    to this.

ICHABOD
Really? That's all I have to do? Shake his hand?

BROM
Insist. Do not take no for an answer. Reach out and grab it
if you have to...
          (demonstrates)
Baltus Van Tassel likes a man who is a man. Who commands
attention and demands friendship. He likes a man to shake his
hand.

ICHABOD
Well, that seems quite simple.

BROM
          (continues to hold onto
          Ichabod's hand as he
          demonstrates)
And when you shake, grasp his hand firmly. Squeeze it.
Squeeze it to within an inch of its life!

ICHABOD
Squeeze?

BROM
Squeeze! And I guarantee you, when you let go of that hand,
you might as well take a look around you at the Van Tassel
home, because it, and his pulchri...pulchri...

ICHABOD
Pulchritudinous...

BROM
Puchritudinous daughter, will inevitably be yours.

ICHABOD
My word! And all I need to do is shake his hand?

BROM
And squeeze.

ICHABOD
Oh, yes, squeeze. I musn't forget to squeeze.

BROM
Squeeze, brother! Squeeze! Now go! And think about how close
you are to becoming Lord of Tarrytown!

ICHABOD
Oh, dear! And I've been here only two weeks!

BROM
Off with you!

ICHABOD
Off with me!

Gleefully, Ichabod races away. Brom
waits a moment, then laughs
uproariously and falls back onto a
bench. Sally approaches him.

SALLY
(playfully)
That was very naughty of you, Brom Bones!

BROM
Ah! So you heard!

SALLY
I did. And both you and I know what is going to happen when
Ichabod Crane takes Baltus Van Tassel hand and shakes it...

BROM
And squeezes!

SALLY
And squeezes!

                    BROM
And squeezes!

                    SALLY
And squeezes!

                    *By now, they are laughing together, as
                    the LIGHTS CHANGE back to the
                    Gossipers.*

                    EMMA
What? What's going to happen???

                    MILLY
              (rising)
Oh, that's enough storytellin' for now. Kate, you want some
rum?

                    KATE
              (also rising)
Never one to turn down some rum.
              (to Emma)
You stay here, Missy. You ain't old enough for rum.

                    EMMA
BUT WHAT HAPPENED TO MR. CRANE WHEN HE MET MR. VAN TASSEL????

                    MILLY
Oh that's right. You arrived late.

                    KATE
You missed it.

                    EMMA
SO WHAT HAPPENED???

                    MILLY
Let us get loosened up a bit.

                    KATE
Yes. The rest of the story will be easier to tell after a
glass or two of rum.

                    MILLY
In the meantime, you keep thinkin' about one word.

                    EMMA
One word?

                    KATE
One word.

                    EMMA
What word? What word should I keep thinking about?

                    *Milly and Kate look at each other, then
                    back at Emma.*

SQUEEZE!!!!!!

MILLY & KATE

The laugh and walk out, leaving Emma speechless.

BLACKOUT

END, ACT ONE

ACT TWO

> *The Gossips. Emma still sits there*
> *stunned from the end of the last act.*
> *Milly and Katie enter, laughing, each*
> *wielding a stein of rum.*

                    MILLY
             (referring to Emma)
Oh, look, Kate! We didn't frighten her away!

                    KATE
We thought all the intrigue in our story would be too much
for ya!

                    MILLY
You bein' so young, and all!
             (sits)

                    KATE
Looks like we gotta take it all the way to the end, Milly.

                    MILLY
Looks like it.

                    KATE
Whatdya say, kiddo? You want the rest of the story?

                    EMMA
Yes!

                    KATE
All right. So guess what we're gonna tell you now?

                    EMMA
What?

                    KATE
             (to Milly)
You tell her.

                    MILLY
You tell her.

                    KATE
I'm not gonna tell her.

                    MILLY
Well, you don't expect me to tell her?

                    EMMA
SOMEBODY TELL ME!

                    KATE
All right. All right. Now we're gonna tell you how Brom Bones
got all caught up with Carlotta Van Derp.

                         EMMA
Finally!

                         MILLY
Well, we needed the rum first.

                         EMMA
Tell me!

                         KATE
All right. Well, the way I heard it...

                    At this point, LIGHTS UP on Brom, off
                    to the side, talking with Ezekiel,
                    seemingly giving him
                    instructions...Kate continues...

                         KATE (cont'd)
...after Brom told the Schoolmaster about Baltus Van Tassel,
he got his henchman, there...the weasel...

                         EMMA
Ezekiel!

                         KATE
That's him! He got him to pass the word all over the village
that Mr. Crane was gonna squeeeeeeze the living daylights
outa Van Tassel's hand.

                         MILLY
AND, he told Ezekiel how he was gonna get all the old ladies
to feel sorry for him for losin' Katrina...

                    Ezekiel and Brom laugh, and the LIGHTS
                    GO OUT on them.

                         EMMA
All the old ladies?

                         MILLY
Yup.

                         EMMA
                    (looks at both Milly and Kate)
Even you?

                    Milly and Kate freeze, and stare Emma
                    down.

                         MILLY
I said OLD ladies!

                         EMMA
Oh. Of course. Go on.

                         MILLY
He was doin' everything he could to get everybody in the
village to turn on the Schoolmaster!

KATE
From what we heard, it was the day before the big sociable at
Baltus Van Tassel's...

MILLY
And there was some strange goin's on at Carlotta's house...

> *Carlotta's den again. Harriet and*
> *Gertrude are there. They stand behind*
> *Carlotta's chair. However, Carlotta is*
> *not in the chair--Brom is. And he's*
> *playing the rejected suitor act to the*
> *hilt, shedding crocodile tears.*

> *The ladies, much like the Giddy Girls,*
> *envelope him, and comfort him in his*
> *misery.*

BROM
(weeping)
Oh, I've lost her forever!!!!

GERTRUDE
Now, now, Brom...

HARRIET
No woman is worth all this misery.

GERTRUDE
She's a mean little vixen, that's all she is!

HARRIET
You should keep company with my daughter, Sally! She'd be
good for you!

BROM
(still wailing)
KATRINA!!!!!

GERTRUDE
My daughter, Maddie would be far better...

HARRIET
Of course, there's also my daughter Ermengarde. But, then,
she does have this big...
(starts to describe
Ermengarde's physical
challenge...)

BROM
(WAILING)
KATRINA!!!!!!!

> *Carlotta enters.*

CARLOTTA
What is going on in here???? It sounds like someone skinning
a pig!

                         BROM
                   (Uh...wailing)
OH! KATRINA LOVES IT WHEN I SKIN THE PIGS!!!!

                       CARLOTTA
OH, BE QUIET, FOR HEAVEN'S SAKE!

                       HARRIET
We have some distressful news, Carlotta.

                       GERTRUDE
Poor Brom is in pain!

                       CARLOTTA
Poor Brom is in my chair!

                         BROM
                    (wailing)
Oh! I am SO SORRY!!!!
                    (he rises)

                       CARLOTTA
Oh, sit down, you fool. Someone tell me what is happening!

                       HARRIET
Well, I got the whole ugly story from my sweet little
AVAILABLE daughter, Sally.

                       CARLOTTA
Give me the short version.

                       GERTRUDE
You're not going to like it.

                       CARLOTTA
I don't like anything. Tell me.

                       GERTRUDE
It's about the Schoolmaster.

                       CARLOTTA
                   (instantly suspicious)
What about the Schoolmaster?

                       HARRIET
He is...
                   (all freeze, waiting for this
                    bombshell to land)

                       GERTRUDE
Go on, Harriet. You can do it.

                       HARRIET
He is...

                       GERTRUDE
I'm here for you...tell her. "He is..."

                         HARRIET
He is...
                  (another pause)
...with woman!

                  Gertrude reacts vocally.

                         CARLOTTA
With...what?

                         GERTRUDE
Woman.

                         CARLOTTA
With...what...woman?

                         BROM
                  (still weeping)
With my woman!

                         GERTRUDE
It's outrageous!

                         HARRIET
It's a sin!

                         GERTRUDE
It's a scandal!

                         BROM
                  (still wailing like a baby)
It's...it's...NOT NICE!

                  He breaks down sobbing. Harriet and
                  Gertrude comfort him again.

                         CARLOTTA
Wait a minute...wait a minute! Are you telling me that
that...that...pusillanimous pedagogue has fallen for Katrina
Van Tassel?

                         HARRIET
Yes!

                         CARLOTTA
Why?

                         BROM
Because she's...she's...pulchritudinous!

                  Again, he breaks down. Again, the
                  ladies comfort him.

                         CARLOTTA
                  (she's had enough)
All right! All right! ALL RIGHT!
                  (to Brom)
You! On your feet!

                        The ladies gently help him to his feet.

                              CARLOTTA (cont'd)
Pull yourself together!

                              GERTRUDE
Carlotta! You must do something about this!

                              HARRIET
We can't have this kind of insubordination!

                              GERTRUDE
Replace the cad immediately!

                              HARRIET
Or sooner!

                              BROM
                         (to Carlotta)
He'll be at the sociable tomorrow night.

                              CARLOTTA
Oh?

                              HARRIET
Sociable?

                              GERTRUDE
What sociable?

                        Harriet and Gertrude question each
                        other "Sociable? What sociable??" and
                        keep at it until...

                              CARLOTTA
QUIET!
                         (everybody stops talking; to
                          Brom, icily)
What...sociable?

                              BROM
                         (with feigned innocence)
Oh. I thought you knew. Katrina and her father have invited
all of...I mean...some of the villagers to their home for a
Halloween sociable tomorrow night. I surely thought you...and
these charming ladies...had been invited...

                        Carlotta looks at the ladies. Each
                        shakes her head, "Not me!"

                              CARLOTTA
                         (sweetly)
I'm sure it's simply an oversight...I'll ask Abigail if the
invitation was in this morning's post...She's taking care of
my niece Felicity this afternoon. I'll call her in.
                         (gently)
Abigail?
                         (a little louder)

CARLOTTA (cont'd)

Abigail.
        (screams)
ABIGAIL!!!!!!

Abigail races in immediately, out of breath, as usual. Felicity is with her, wearing a jacket, ready to leave.

ABIGAIL

Yes! Yes! Yes! I'm here! I hope I didn't make you wait!
        (beat)
Miss Felicity is ready for you to take her home now. You see, I....

CARLOTTA

Abigail...was there an invitation in today's post for me?

ABIGAIL

Invitation?

CARLOTTA

Yes, Abigail. An invitation. It's a letter, and in the letter there is...

ABIGAIL
        (removes letter from apron)
You mean this, Miss?

CARLOTTA

Ah! There! You see! I <u>have</u> been invited!

ABIGAIL

Oh! You have! Isn't that wonderful! Now we can go together!

CARLOTTA
        (again, icily)
What?

ABIGAIL

Well, I have this invitation which was sent to me, so that means we can...

CARLOTTA

Abigail...was that...the only...invitation...in the post?

ABIGAIL
        (beginning to sense the
        awfulness; speaks normally)
Oh.
        (then, with elevated surprise)
Oh!
        (then, with extreme dread)
Oh.

CARLOTTA

Abigail...?

                    ABIGAIL
I'm afraid to answer.

                    CARLOTTA
          (beat)
I see.
          (another beat)
Abigail...

                    ABIGAIL
Yes, Miss?

                    CARLOTTA
Read the invitation.

                    ABIGAIL
Read it?

                    CARLOTTA
Read it.

                    Abigail starts to read the invitation
                    silently, moving her lips.

                    CARLOTTA (cont'd)
Abigail?

                    ABIGAIL
Yes. Miss?

                    CARLOTTA
Aloud.

                    ABIGAIL
Oh. Yes.
          (reads)
"To Miss Abigail Van Derlay...You and a guest are cordially
invited to..."

                    CARLOTTA
That's enough! Abigail...thank you so much. I would be happy
to accompany you to the sociable tomorrow night. As your
guest.

                    ABIGAIL
Oh. So you'll be the guest?

                    CARLOTTA
Yes. In fact...we all will be your guest!

                    The ladies nod in approval.

                    ABIGAIL
Oh. Well...that's almost...more joy...than I could ever...

                    CARLOTTA
Abigail?

                        ABIGAIL
Yes, Miss?

                        CARLOTTA
You may leave now.

                        ABIGAIL
Yes, Miss.
            (starts out)

                        CARLOTTA
Oh, Abigail?

                        ABIGAIL
            (stops)
Yes, Miss?

                        CARLOTTA
Have I ever told you how much I appreciate all the things you
do for me?

                        ABIGAIL
            (beat; smiles in anticipation)
No, Miss.

                        CARLOTTA
            (beat)
That's a shame.
            (long beat)
That will be all!

                        Abigail leaves. Felicity stays.
                        Carlotta instantly turns to the ladies.

                        CARLOTTA (cont'd)
Thank you, ladies. I have business with Mr. Van Brunt, here.

                        HARRIET
Carlotta, would you like us to stay?

                        CARLOTTA
No.

                        GERTRUDE
Are you sure?

                        CARLOTTA
Am I ever...unsure?

                        HARRIET
We'll see you at the sociable!

                        GERTRUDE
I hope I can find something to wear!

                        HARRIET
As long as you don't wear that!

Harriet and Gertrude leave. Carlotta is
left alone with Brom. Felicity stands,
patiently waiting.

                    CARLOTTA
              (to Felicity)
You just sit, Felicity. I'll take you home presently. I don't
know why your parents leave you with me!

                    FELICITY
              (cheerily sitting)
Nor do I!

                    CARLOTTA
              (to Brom)
As for you...You can't fool me. Those were crocodile tears.
You have something up your sleeve.

                    BROM
And what if I do? Why should he swoop into town and take
Katrina's love from me?

                    CARLOTTA
Don't you mean Katrina's inheritance?

                    BROM
Inheritance...Love...six of one...

                    CARLOTTA
Let's face it. We want the same thing. We want him out of
town. To think that he disobeyed my orders!

                    BROM
Well, I've done what I can. It won't be easy. Even for you.
The Schoolmaster seems to have somehow charmed everybody in
the village. The ladies love him, the wastrels love him, the
children love him...

                    CARLOTTA
              (to Felicity)
Is that true?

                    FELICITY
The Schoolmaster! Oh, yes! He's very, very nice.

                    CARLOTTA
He MUST have an Achilles Heel!

                    BROM
Something that...phases him...that bothers
him...that...that...

                    FELICITY
Frightens him?

                    CARLOTTA
              (beat)
Yes. Frightens him.

                         CARLOTTA (cont'd)
                    (beat)
          Why? Do you...know something we don't know...?

                         FELICITY
                    (coyly)
          Perhaps.

                         CARLOTTA
          Oh?

                         FELICITY
          And perhaps...I will tell you what I know that will frighten
          the Schoolmaster...if...

                         CARLOTTA
          If...?

                         FELICITY
          If...you promise to have Abigail bake me a batch of those
          lovely oatmeal cookies every time I come here to visit.

                         CARLOTTA
          But Felicity...you know your parents forbade my allowing that
          when you became so sick the last time...

                         FELICITY
          I know.

                         CARLOTTA
          Felicity...that is devious, deceitful, underhanded, low and
          downright nasty of you.
                    (beat; embraces Felicity)
          My own flesh and blood! Tell us!

                         FELICITY
          Well, you see, the other day in the schoolroom...

                         *Carlotta and Brom listen intently as
                         the LIGHTS CHANGE back to the Gossips.*

                         MILLY
          And this is all true!

                         KATE
          We heard the whole story from Felicity the day after the
          sociable.

                         MILLY
          The little brat can't keep her mouth shut.

                         EMMA
          What did she tell them?

                         KATE
          Well, we're not quite sure. But we have a pretty good idea.

                         EMMA
          I thought you said Felicity told you the whole story.

                         MILLY
Oh, we never get the whole whole story.

                         KATE
Never.

                         MILLY
We always have to make up a little on our own.

                         KATE
Keeps us on our toes.

                         EMMA
So what happened next?

                         KATE
Well, next came the sociable. And you were there. Eventually.

                         MILLY
We were all there!

                         EMMA
But I didn't notice anything...

                         KATE
That's because you don't know what to notice yet.

                         EMMA
But you do?

                         MILLY & KATE
YES!

                         EMMA
Well, what did you notice?

                         KATE
Oh...when I think what might have happened to poor Mr.
Crane...

                         MILLY
Poor dead Mr. Crane.

                         KATE
He ain't dead!

                         MILLY
Then where is he?

                         KATE
Nobody knows!

                         MILLY
I know! He's murdered!

                         KATE
He ain't murdered!

                    MILLY
He's dead, ain't he?

                    KATE
Yes. NO!

                    MILLY
Aha!

                    EMMA
PLEASE!
          (beat)
Just tell me what you think happened...

                              The LIGHTS CHANGE to the Van Tassel
                              farmhouse, decked out for the sociable.

                              At rise, all the wastrels and Giddy
                              Girls are there. Bessie is there, too,
                              playing fiddle, accompanied by Henry on
                              some kind of tympani instrument. The
                              schoolchildren are there. Milly, Kate
                              and Emma are there. Everybody is
                              dancing to Bessie's fiddle playing. as
                              the participants are dancing.

                              Seated in the midst of all of this in a
                              large chair is Baltus VAN TASSEL,
                              Katrina's father, and lord of the
                              manor. He is large and loud and full of
                              energy. As he sits, his feet tap and he
                              claps in rhythm to the music. Next to
                              him stands Katrina, not dancing at the
                              moment, but enjoying the festivities.

                              This revelry goes on for a few minutes,
                              and everybody is having a wonderful
                              time.

                              As the music continues, Van Tassel
                              bellows to his daughter!

                    VAN TASSEL
What a delightful group of people you've invited, daughter!

                    KATRINA
And there's more to arrive, Father!

                    VAN TASSEL
Wonderful! If only your mother were still here, how she would
enjoy all this!

                    KATRINA
She certainly loved the farm.

                    VAN TASSEL
And someday, my dear, when I'm gone, all this will be yours!

KATRINA

Oh, father, don't talk that way!

VAN TASSEL

We must be practical, Katrina! We must find you a suitable
husband and you and he can share my wealth!

KATRINA
(pleasantly)

Oh, father, stop!

> At this point, Brom enters with
> Ezekiel. The Giddy Girls swarm around
> Brom and bring him into the dance.
> Ezekiel does what he can to fend them
> off, but fails, and ends up dancing
> himself.

VAN TASSEL
(indicating Brom)

Now that Van Brunt fellow, there. He's the kind of man I want
for you!

KATRINA
(coyly)

But, Father, you haven't met the Schoolmaster!

VAN TASSEL

Oh, the Schoolmaster, no, no, no! I've seen him around and
about. No. I want a real man for my daughter!

KATRINA
(again, coyly)

We'll see, Father. We'll see...

> As the music and dancing continue, the
> students congregate to one side,
> brought together by Felicity.

FELICITY

Has anybody seen the Schoolmaster?

DOROTHY

I heard he borrowed the Van Fenster plow horse to ride here.

LENORA

Oh, no! Not Gunpowder!

GEORGE

That means he'll arrive late.

LENORA

Or never.

FELICITY

Well, when he does get here, he is in for a big surprise!

                    DOROTHY
What surprise?

                    BENJAMIN
What are you talking about?

                    FELICITY
I promised I wouldn't tell!

                    GEORGE
But you have to tell us!

                    LENORA
We're your best friends in the whole, complete world.

                    GEORGE
That's redundant.

                    LENORA
I know!
          (she doesn't)

                    DOROTHY
Please tell us!

                    GEORGE
Please!

                    LENORA
Tell us...PLEASE!!!!

                    FELICITY
          (beat)
Well...since my Aunt Carlotta told me not to tell...I'll
tell!

                    BENJAMIN
          (annoyed)
WHAT!!!

                              Giggling (except for Benjamin), the
                              students disappear into the crowd as
                              Felicity tells them her secret.

                              As the music continues, Brom breaks
                              away from the dance for a moment, and
                              pulls Ezekiel away with him.

                    BROM
Ezekiel...did you...take care of that...chore I asked you to
take care of?

                    EZEKIEL
Well, it wasn't easy, but I got it done.

                    BROM
Good. Where did you put it?

                         EZEKIEL
In the barn, in back of the big hayloft.

                         BROM
Excellent. Excellent. Now...go out and make certain Daredevil
is ready...

                         EZEKIEL
Are you sure about this?

                         BROM
I'm sure. Go!

                         Ezekiel leaves the dance. The Giddy
                         Girls break away from the dance and
                         surround Brom, and each tries to grab
                         hold of his arm as they speak...
                         SALLY
Brom! You mustn't run off like that!

                         JESSIE
In the middle of the dance!

                         MADDIE
It was my turn to spin with you!

                         LIZZIE
                    (to Maddie)
You spun already! I saw you!

                         HANNAH
                    (to Maddie)
You can't spin twice!

                         MADDIE
Sally spun twice!

                         SALLY
I always spin twice! That's because Brom likes the way I
spin, don't you Brom!

                         As a group, they drag him back into the
                         dance. He goes willingly.

                         Felicity has finished telling her plan
                         to the school children. They are
                         excited.

                         GEORGE
Boy! Now, that's what I call a plan!

                         LENORA
What a great idea!

                         BENJAMIN
But...he can't do that!

                        FELICITY
Says who?

                        BENJAMIN
Says...social consciousness!

                        FELICITY
How would you like me to give you a little social
consciousness right in the nose!
                    (fist in his face)

                        BENJAMIN
But Brom just can't do something like that! It's rude and
mean and terrible and awful and it flies in the face of
civility and good manners!

                        DOROTHY
Yeah, but it's fun.

                All the kids agree.

                        BENJAMIN
Well, you won't get away with it! I'm going to tell the
Schoolmaster!

                He runs off.

                        FELICITY
Dorothy.

                        DOROTHY
Yo!

                        FELICITY
You can catch up to him, right?

                        DOROTHY
Absolutely.

                        FELICITY
Good. You know what to do.

                        DOROTHY
Absolutely.

                        FELICITY
Go.

                Dorothy runs off after Benjamin.

                        GEORGE
Wow! She's fast!

                        LENORA
What's she gonna do?

                        FELICITY
You don't want to know.

The kids ease into the crowd.

Carlotta enters with Harriet and Gertrude. Abigail brings up the rear.

Carlotta is instantly annoyed. She puts her hands to her ears.

                    CARLOTTA
Sweet Mother of...noise! What is this infernal noise?
ABIGAIL! You didn't say there would be...noise!

                    ABIGAIL
Noise is part of the fun, Miss. There's always fun at
parties.

                    CARLOTTA
Not at MY parties!

                    ABIGAIL
I know, Miss.

                    CARLOTTA
Never mind. Take our wraps and...do something with them!

                    ABIGAIL
Yes, Miss.

Abigail gathers the ladies' shawls while Carlotta gives her silent instructions.

Van Tassel calls for his daughter.

                    VAN TASSEL
Katrina!

                    KATRINA
               (comes to him)
Yes, Father?

                    VAN TASSEL
What are those...women doing here?

                    KATRINA
I don't know, Father. I certainly didn't invite them!

                    VAN TASSEL
You know how much I dislike them. All of them!

                    KATRINA
I do, Father...

                    CARLOTTA
               (seeing Van Tassel, calling)
Oh, Baltus Van Tassel! It's been such a long time!
               (she heads over to him)

                              VAN TASSEL
                    (under his breath, to Katrina)
          Oh, good Lord, not her...Find out how this happened!
                    (changes attitude; to Carlotta)
          Carlotta!!!!

                              Carlotta and Van Tassel enter into
                              conversation. Katrina moves to Abigail.

                              KATRINA
                    (calls)
          Oh, Abigail?

                              ABIGAIL
                    (now carrying the shawls)
          Yes...Yes, Katrina?
                    (she and Katrina meet)

                              KATRINA
          Abigail...why is Carlotta here?

                              ABIGAIL
          I'm so sorry, Katrina! She found out about the sociable and
          bullied her way in, as usual.

                              KATRINA
          My father is not pleased.

                              ABIGAIL
          Are you going to throw her out, Miss?

                              KATRINA
          Well, I...

                              ABIGAIL
          If you do, it's all right with me. Just don't tell her I said
          so!

                              KATRINA
          I'm not going to throw her out, Abigail.

                              ABIGAIL
          Oh. I see. Well...another moment of hope dashed.

                              She goes off with the shawls.

                              As she does, Ichabod enters. Katrina
                              sees him. But just as she does...Brom
                              sweeps over to Katrina, and sweeps her
                              into the dance.

                              Ichabod, a bit bedraggled because of
                              his horse ride, finds himself standing
                              with Carlotta's ladies.

*Carlotta sees that Ichabod has arrived,
and excuses herself from Van Tassel,
making her way over to Ichabod during
the next few lines...*

HARRIET

Well, look what the cat dragged in!

ICHABOD

Excuse me!

GERTRUDE

There is no excuse for you!

HARRIET

You smell, sir!

ICHABOD

Well, you see, I had to borrow ...

HARRIET

What is that odor?

GERTRUDE
(sniffing)
Horse. I believe it is horse!

ICHABOD

It is horse. I had to borrow the Van Fenster's...

HARRIET
(as Carlotta arrives)
Carlotta! This man smells like horse!

ICHABOD

Miss Van Derp, there is something I'd like to...

CARLOTTA

Schoolmaster! How wonderful that you're here! Let me
introduce you to Mr. Van Tassel...

ICHABOD

Yes, that would be nice, but before we do, may I tell you...

CARLOTTA

Oh, Baltus! Baltus! Would you come here, please?

*Baltus rises and heads toward Carlotta
and Ichabod.*

*Brom goes over to Bessie, who is still
fiddling. He's dragging Katrina with
him.*

BROM

Bessie! Would you rest for a moment, please?

BESSIE

What? Rest? You know me, once I get goin' there's no stoppin'
me! Once I get goin', I go all the way!

HENRY
(almost to himself)
Ain't that the truth...

BROM

Please, Bessie...just a few minutes...

BESSIE

Ah, all right. HENRY! Get me a rum!

HENRY
(mumbles, as he moves away)
Come, sweet death...

> The Giddy Girls and wastrels are in on
> Brom's plan. The students watch with
> interest. Most everybody has an idea
> about what Brom is up to.

BROM
(pulls Katrina to where she can
see)
Oh...you must see this!

JEB

Oh, it's time for the squeeze!

SUSANNAH

This is going to be fun!

WEED

I don't know. I think it's kind of mean.

JEB

Oh, don't be a jellyfish!

WEED

What's a jellyfish?

SUSANNAH

It's a fish made out of jelly! Ssh!

> Baltus has reached Ichabod and
> Carlotta.

CARLOTTA

Baltus Van Tassel, I would like you to meet our new
Schoolmaster...Ichabod Crane.

> Ichabod looks to Brom, who smiles and
> gives him an encouraging gesture about
> squeezing.

                         ICHABOD
Mr. Van Tassel, I can't tell you what it pleasure it is to
meet you!

                         He holds out his hand. Van Tassel looks
                         at it, but does not take it.

                         VAN TASSEL
Well, my boy, you see, I never...

                         Ichabod reaches down and grabs Van
                         Tassel's right hand. He pulls it up and
                         begins shaking it vigorously. Van
                         Tassel reacts very badly.

                         After some serious shaking, Ichabod
                         stops, but keeps holding the hand,
                         which he begins to squeeze....and
                         squeeze.....and squeeze...the crowd of
                         people in the know can barely hold back
                         their laughter...

                         Van Tassel is more and more in pain
                         until he can't take it any longer...

                         VAN TASSEL (cont'd)
MY...GOOD....MAN!!!!

                         ICHABOD
Oh! I'm glad you like it, sir. Let me squeeze a little
harder...

                         He does. Van Tassel wails in pain...

                         VAN TASSEL
KA...TRI...NAAAAAAAAAAA!

                         He yanks his hand away from Ichabod.
                         Katrina runs over to him. She senses
                         what Brom has done, and gives him a
                         very angry look. She brings her father
                         back to his chair.

                         VAN TASSEL (cont'd)
He....He...squeezed!

                         The crowd laughs. The ladies are
                         shocked. Ichabod is humiliated and very
                         confused. Henry steps up. Bessie is now
                         drinking heartily.

                         HENRY
All right, let's give Bessie a few moments to...relax.
                    (he looks at her, she takes a
                       big swig)
Everybody enjoy the refreshments and get ready for
storytelling!

There is a smattering of applause as
the crowd disperses to various parts of
the room. Ezekiel returns. Emma arrives
and scoots over to the Gossips.

Katrina goes to Brom, who is still
swamped by the giggling Giddy Girls.

KATRINA

Abraham Van Brunt, that was a terrible thing to do! You know
Father hates to be touched.

BROM

That Schoolmaster got what he deserved!

SALLY

I've never laughed so much in my life!

KATRINA

Well, I don't think it was very funny.

And she walks briskly away, and goes to
Ichabod to comfort him.

EZEKIEL

I thought it was most amusing.

BROM
(astonished; aware of Katrina
and Ichabod)

Well, would you look at that!

JESSIE

Come on, Brom, let's have some punch.

BROM

I'd like to give somebody a punch.

EZEKIEL

Just tell me who, Brom!

BROM

Heel, Ezekiel.

EZEKIEL

Right!

BROM

Is everything ready?

EZEKIEL

Ready!

BROM

Good!

MADDIE

Are you going to tell a story tonight, Brom?

LIZZIE

You're the best storyteller in the village!

HANNAH

No! In the county!

> Carlotta has wormed her way into the
> group.

CARLOTTA

Oh, he'll be telling a story tonight...won't you Brom?

BROM

Yes.
> (determined)

Oh, yes!
> (to girls)

Listen...when Henry calls for the storyteller, I want you all
to make sure he chooses me. Will you do that?

SALLY

Of course we'll do that! Is there anything we won't do for
you, Brom?

BROM

I guess not...go...get ready!

> The Giddy Girls giggle and move away.
> Brom returns his focus to Katrina, who
> is still comforting Ichabod.

BROM (cont'd)

Look at the way she's tending to him. Like he's her long lost
puppy.

EZEKIEL

I hate puppies.

CARLOTTA
> (to Brom)

You know what you have to do.

BROM

I do. I absolutely do.

CARLOTTA

Have you made the proper arrangements?

BROM

I have!

EZEKIEL

We have!

CARLOTTA
> (to Ezekiel)

Who are you?

                         EZEKIEL
I'm Brom's...Brom's...to tell you the truth, I don't know
what I am.

                         BROM
Never mind him. I'm ready.

                         CARLOTTA
Good. Let's just hope you're up to the task.

                         BROM
                    (beat)
Just...watch me.

               Henry takes the stage again.

                         HENRY
All right, let's all gather 'round for the Halloween
storyteller. Who will it be this year?

                         *There is a big cry for "Brom! Brom
                         Bones!" Once the wastrels see the
                         intensity of the Giddy Girls cry for
                         Brom, they join in as well.*

                         HENRY (cont'd)
                    (not thrilled)
Are you sure?

                    Another huge roar for Brom!

                         HENRY (cont'd)
All right, if we must. Brom Bones? Do you have a story to
tell?

                         BROM
                    (moves to the center)
Well, Henry...I think I might be able to come up with
something!

                    Another big cheer for "Brom!"

                         BROM (cont'd)
Snuggle up close to each other, folks...Nobody should be
alone when I tell this story...

                         *Some folks snuggle up. Jeb tries to
                         snuggle up to Jessie.*

                         JESSIE
Hey! Watch where you're snugglin'!

                         JEB
Sorry. I thought you were Weed.

                         WEED
What?

                    ICHABOD
            (to Katrina, as he moves in to
            her a bit)
Do you mind?

                    KATRINA
            (a bit taken aback)
Um...no...

                    VAN TASSEL
            (from across the room)
Watch out for him, daughter! He squeezes!

                    KATRINA
I'll be fine, Father. Just listen to the story.

                    BROM
Susannah, would you...bring a couple of the lamps down a bit?

            *Susannah goes to a lamp or two and
            lowers the lights.*

                    BROM (cont'd)
That's better. Want to make sure we have the right mood...
            (clears his throat)
Tonight...I will tell the story...of Major Andre!

            *There is a gasp from the crowd. The
            children scream and huddle together...*

                    ICHABOD
            (to Katrina)
Major Andre?

                    KATRINA
Oh, dear...

                    ICHABOD
Oh, dear? Why oh, dear?

                    VAN TASSEL
            (rises)
My boy...don't you think that story is a bit...too...

                    BROM
No, sir, I do not. When better than Halloween night to tell
the story of...The Headless Horseman!

            Ichabod squeaks. Van Tassel sits.

                    ICHABOD
            (his voice still in squeak
            mode)
Headless...Horseman?

                    KATRINA
            (to Brom)
Brom...what do you think you're doing.

                    BROM
Oh, I'm sorry. Would the Schoolmaster prefer I tell a gentler
story? "Mary Had A Little Lamb" perhaps?

                    Laughs from most of the folks.

                    ICHABOD
Uh...no...no...just...go ahead with your...your...

                    BROM
Headless Horseman story?

                    ICHABOD
Yes. That one. Yes.
          (to Katrina)
Where is the outbuilding...just in case...

                    KATRINA
Oh, Mr. Crane...

                    BROM
          (really gets into the story, as
          it proceeds)
It was near the end of the war, the war in which we earned
our freedom from the shackles of the King of England, the war
which saw so many of our Colonial lads meet their maker at
the hands of the heartless, bloody Redcoats!

                    ICHABOD
          (listens to every word, reacts
          instinctively)
Ooooh...they met their maker...

                    BROM
And, of course, the Redcoats didn't find the battle worthy
enough to fight us on their own. No! They had to enlist the
service of Hessian soldiers, who were paid to come here from
Germany! Mercenaries who fought us and killed us solely to
pad their German pockets!

                    ICHABOD
          (again, scared to death)
Killed us. They killed us...

                    BROM
And the most vicious, the most bloodthirsty, the most vile,
cruel and murderous of all these Hessian soldiers was the
notorious...Major Andre!

                    ICHABOD
          (to Katrina, as he rises and
          moves to another part of the
          room)
I think I need to walk...Yes, I need to walk...Walk...I'm
walking....

                    He heads toward one of the exits.
                    Ezekiel blocks his way.

CARLOTTA
What's the matter, Schoolmaster?

ICHABOD
Well, you know, I was thinking...I might want to start back
early, you know...to prepare my lesson for...

CARLOTTA
But there is no school tomorrow. Isn't that right?

The students all confirm this.

BROM
No school! You have all the time in the world! Sit,
Schoolmaster! Sit and listen to the rest of the story!

ICHABOD
Well...you see, I...I...

EZEKIEL
SIDDOWN!

Ezekiel slams Ichabod into a seat.

ICHABOD
I'm sitting. I'm sitting. Not scared. Sitting.

EZEKIEL
Go ahead, Brom!

BROM
And you all know about the battle that took place down by the
creek on Halloween night! You all know that our brave
colonials defeated the Hessian mob and drove them from the
county. And you all know...you all know...what happened to
Major Andre!

*The Giddy Girls shout..."No! No! Tell
us, Brom! Tell us what happened!"*

BROM (cont'd)
Are you sure?

Again, more "Tell us! Tell us!"

ICHABOD
Oh, I don't know if that's necessary...

BROM
All right...I'll tell you...

ICHABOD
Oh, dear...

*As Ichabod listens to the rest of this
story, he grows more visibly upset and
frightened, rising from his seat,
displaying abject fear in his face.*

                              BROM
The Major knew defeat was imminent. Desiring to live to
murder and loot another day, he led his men into retreat,
riding his enormous black steed through the glen and into the
hollow. But just as he was about to cross the footbridge
which would assure his escape, a cannonball shrieked towards
him. He heard the blast, but didn't have time to elude the
fiery missle. It struck him square on the head, ripping his
skull from his neck, cleanly separating it from his three-
corner hat! Without their leader, the rest of his men
continued over the bridge, and down the county road, never to
be seen again. And Major Andre...or what was left of Major
Andre...was buried in the church yard, and his bones have
stayed there to this very day.

                            ICHABOD
                    (quickly, dismissively)
Ah. Well. Very good story. I think I'll just...

                              BROM
HOWEVER...

                            ICHABOD
Oh, dear. There's a "however..."

                              BROM
However...as you all know...the story has come down through
the years that the spirit...the ghost...of Major Andre haunts
the glen at night...the glen that some of you...will pass
through on your way home...

                            ICHABOD
Me, right?

                              BROM
Yes, you, Schoolmaster...the story is told that the vicious
Major rides up and down the hollow leading to the glen,
looking...searching...for his long...lost...

                            ICHABOD
Oh, dear, not his head...don't say his head...

                              BROM
Head! And the story continues...

                            ICHABOD
Oh, God, the story continues...

                              BROM
If the Major happens to see anyone as he roams the
hollow...that person...
                    (looks at Ichabod)
...whoever he may be...he'd better ride...

                            ICHABOD
Ride...

                              BROM
Like his life depended on it...

                              ICHABOD
Oooh...

                              BROM
Becasue it DOES! So ride fast!

                              ICHABOD
Ride fast...

                              BROM
                          (acts this out)
Because if the Major catches you, he will grab his sword...

                              ICHABOD
Oh, not his sword...

                              BROM
And slash your head off at the neck, and take it for his own!

                    Ichabod shrieks again.

                              BROM (cont'd)
But never fear...

                              ICHABOD
Too late...

                              BROM
There is one way to escape!

                              ICHABOD
Oh, thank heavens...

                              BROM
You must ride!

                              ICHABOD
I got that. Ride. Been riding...

                              BROM
And ride fast!

                              ICHABOD
Noted. Yes. Fast. Riding fast.

                              BROM
And you must reach the bridge that spans the brook! Because
when you reach that bridge...

                              ICHABOD
When I reach it? Yes? Yes?

                              BROM
You must traverse!

                         ICHABOD
I must?

                         BROM
YOU MUST!

                         ICHABOD
Oh, I will! I WILL!

                         BROM
For once you traverse the bridge...the Major's power...is no
more!

                         ICHABOD
Oh, that is wonderful news...

                         BROM
Of course...this is all a legend...

                         ICHABOD
A legend.

                         BROM
It may not be true.

                         ICHABOD
No?

                         BROM
It probably isn't true!

                         ICHABOD
Oh!

                         BROM
I mean...to my knowledge...no one has ever encountered the
ghost of the Major.

                         ICHABOD
Well, then...why am I all...

                         BROM
                    (in Ichabod's face)
And LIVED!

                              This petrifies Ichabod to the point
                              where he can't even speak. Again, he
                              squeaks. Brom knows he has achieved his
                              goal. He smiles, and turns back to the
                              rest of the group.

                         BROM (cont'd)
And that...my good friends...is my Halloween story!

                              He bows and the crowd applauds. Brom
                              goes back over to Ichabod. Carlotta
                              joins him.

BROM (cont'd)
Why, Schoolmaster...you're looking a little peaked.

ICHABOD
I am?

CARLOTTA
A little green around the gills...

ICHABOD
I have gills?

BROM
Katrina...
(she steps over to them)
Doesn't the Schoolmaster look a little peaked?

KATRINA
I shouldn't be surprised, after listening to that
ridiculous...

ICHABOD
Oh, no, Katrina! Don't say that! We mustn't risk waking the
spirits by disbelieving in them.

BROM
Oh, we definitely mustn't! I think you should head back to
the Ven Fenster farm and get to bed.

KATRINA
Oh, Brom...

ICHABOD
(looking at Katrina)
But...but I wanted to...to dance with...

CARLOTTA
Oh, no! No dancing! Get home!

VAN TASSEL
(bursts into the group, holding
his hand)
Yes! Home! You'd better go home! Safer for all of us!

KATRINA
Maybe you should, Icky. There'll only be more trouble here.

VAN TASSEL
(to himself)
Icky?

ICHABOD
Well...if you think I should.

KATRINA
I do.

                    ICHABOD
Well...then...I bid you all...farewell.
                    (moves to door)
Until the next time.
                    (another move to door)

                    CARLOTTA
If there is...a next time!

                         Ichabod giggles with phony
                         bravado...and leaves.

                    VAN TASSEL
Henry! Bessie! Music! This is supposed to be a festive
evening! Everybody! Enjoy!
                    (looks to Katrina)
Did you see what he did to my hand?

                         Whining, he and Katrina go back to
                         where he was sitting.

                         Henry and Bessie go back to playing.
                         The Giddy Girls swarm around Brom
                         again, congratulating him for his
                         story.

                    BROM
All right, girls! There's more fun to come! Children! Come
over here! Jeb! Weed! Susannah! You, too!
                    (they join the group)
Now...I have some plans for the rest of the night's
frivolity! And I need you to help. Listen...

                         He huddles them around him. Ezekiel
                         stands on the perimeter and guards.
                         Abigail tries to insinuate herself into
                         the group, but doesn't succeed.

                         Harriet and Gertrude surround Carlotta.

                    GERTRUDE
What is he up to?

                    HARRIET
                    (pleasantly)
No good! I'm sure!

                    GERTRUDE
He's such a scamp!

                    HARRIET
Do you know what he's planning, Carlotta?

                    CARLOTTA
Perhaps.

                    GERTRUDE
Will you tell us?

                    CARLOTTA
              (sinisterly)
Oh...use your imaginations!
              (sees Abigail, gently)
Abigail?
              (Abigail doesn't notice, keeps
              trying to get into the group;
              a little louder)
Abigail...
              (again, no response, screams)
ABIGAIL!

                    Abigail instantly leaves the group, and
                    runs over to Carlotta.

                    ABIGAIL
Yes, Miss!

                    CARLOTTA
Prepare the coach.
              (beat)
Our work here is done!

                    She pushes Abigail to the door, then
                    sweeps out behind her, with the other
                    ladies scurrying after them.

                    BROM
              (to the group)
Does everybody undertand what you have to do?

                    Everybody in his group agrees. Ezekiel
                    speaks over the agreement.

                    EZEKIEL
Everybody understand, Brom!

                    BROM
Thank you, Ezekiel. Well, then...follow me!

                    He leads the all out the door. Henry,
                    sensing trouble, stops playing. Bessie
                    keeps playing.

                    HENRY
Bones!
              (runs after them)
What are you up to?
              (leaves behind them)
BONES!

                    Benjamin then races in, with a gag in
                    his mouth. He is tied to a fencepost,
                    which he has removed from the ground,
                    and has hauled with him in his escape.

> *He approaches the Gossips, who simply point, as one, to where Brom and the others left. Benjamin follows. With the gag. And the fence post.*
>
> *The Gossips, of course, have watched all the goings on.*

                    EMMA
What's the matter with Henry?

                    KATE
Tell her!

                    MILLY
              (rises to leave)
I'm not tellin' her...

                    KATE
              (also rises)
Well, I'm not tellin' her...

                    MILLY
              (starts out)
If you think I'm gonna tell her...

                    KATE
              (goes with her)
Well, you know I'm not tellin' her...

                    EMMA
              (runs after them)
SOMEBODY TELL ME!!!

> *And they are gone.*

                    VAN TASSEL
              (still whining, holding his
              hand)
Oh, daughter...I'm in such pain...

                    KATRINA
              (he's such a baby)
Oh, Father....

                    VAN TASSEL
Take me to my room! I must lie down!

                    KATRINA
Certainly, Father...

                    VAN TASSEL
              (as they leave, stops; very
              whiny)
I could...I could die!

                              KATRINA
                       (they continue out)
Yes, Father...

                       Katrina leads Van Tassel away, with him
                       whimpering all the way.

                       Bessie is left alone, playing the
                       fiddle ferociously. She recognizes that
                       there is nobody in the room but her.

                       She plays louder, with more energy,
                       smiles, moves into the room, and really
                       gets into the song.

                       As the song gets more energized, the
                       LIGHTS go to black.

                       LIGHTS UP on Gossips.

                              EMMA
But we left the sociable! How do you know what happened to
Mr. Crane...

                              MILLY
Well, from here on in, it's all speculation.

                              KATE
She has her ideas. I have mine.

                              EMMA
What ideas?

                              MILLY
Murder!

                              KATE
There wasn't no murder!

                              MILLY
You don't know what you're talkin' about.

                              KATE
Oh, and you do?

                              MILLY
I do.

                              EMMA
But you said it was speculation. How could you know?

                              MILLY
Well, I know what I'm speculatin' about.

                              KATE
All right...so go ahead...go ahead and speculate...

MILLY
Well...when the Schoolmaster left the sociable, he got on his
horse, or whatever you call that Gunpowder thing, and headed
back to the Van Fenster farm...

EMMA
Through the glen?

KATE
It's the only way to get there. Unless you use the rowboat.

MILLY
There's a hole in the rowboat.

KATE
Like I said, the only way to get there is through the
glen...and over the bridge...

MILLY
So off he went, into the night...

> It is night, in the glen. SOUNDS of the
> night--crickets, wind, rustling trees--
> pervade the atmosphere.
>
> The stage is bare, except for Ichabod,
> center, on a horse. (Perhaps a saw
> horse with a saddle. Don't put a horse
> head on it--let the audience imagine
> it's a real horse...)
>
> We hear the very slow CLIP CLOP of the
> horse as Ichabod, frigntened out of his
> wits, plops along.
>
> Eerie music also accompanies this
> scene.
>
> (The scene proceeds and includes the
> term SCARY SOUND to indicate a moment
> when some kind of spine-tingling sound
> comes from the forest. Since this scene
> has been set up with Brom and the
> wastrels and the Giddy Girls and the
> school children having left the
> sociable as a group, these scary
> sounds, while eerie, can also have a
> human sound to them, since it will be
> these people who are providing them,
> unseen, with the intent of frightening
> Ichabod...)
>
> Ichabod proceeds carefully, looking to
> the right and the left, just praying to
> get through the glen and make it to the
> bridge...

                         ICHABOD
                (tentatively, to the horse)
Steady on, Gunpowder. Only a few miles to go before we get to
the bridge...
                    (listless WHINNY from
                    Gunpowder)
Gunpowder...wonder what they were drinking when they gave you
that name...should have called you Sleepwalker...
                    (angry WHINNY from Gunpowder as
                    Ichabod rustles in the saddle)
All right, all right...don't get snitty with me...we'll be
back to the farm before you know it...

                         He clops along, looking to the right
                         and the left...

                         Suddenly, there is a SCARY SOUND from
                         the forest...Ichabod reacts...

                         ICHABOD (cont'd)
Oh, dear, oh, dear, oh, dear...I never should have listened
to those spooky stories...Of course, they're
just....stories...aren't they?...Look who I'm talking to...a
dumb animal...
                    (another annoyed WHINNY from
                    Gunpowder)
My, you are touchy, aren't you?

                         They clop along. From the forest, way
                         off in the distance...we hear the
                         plaintive, but spooky sounds of VOICES
                         saying...

                         "Ichabod....Ichabod....Ichabod..."

                         Ichabod kicks Gunpowder, and the clip
                         clops accelerate...

                         ICHABOD (cont'd)
The wind is certainly playing tricks with me tonight...come
on, Gunpowder, live up to your name!

                         The cries of "Ichabod" increase in
                         volume and are now joined by HAUNTING
                         LAUGHS coming from all sides of
                         Ichabod's head. We can probably
                         recognize CARLOTTA'S CACKLE in the
                         noise. Ichabod kicks Gunpowder to pick
                         up the pace...

                         ICHABOD (cont'd)
I don't find anything funny about this! Where is that god
forsaken bridge!!!

                         The sounds of the CLIP CLOPS have
                         picked up. More SCARY SOUNDS come from
                         the forest, aimed from all sides at
                         Ichabod.

The MUSIC is beginning to build.
Ichabod is kicking Gunpowder who seems
to be getting faster and faster.
Ichabod looks to the skies as all this
happens.

ICHABOD (cont'd)
OH, PLEASE LET ME GET TO THE BRIDGE BEFORE IT'S TOO LATE!!!!

The NOISES and the MUSIC build and
build...the CLIP CLOPS of Gunpowder get
faster and louder...

Suddenly, eclipsing all of this, comes
the HORRIFYING ROAR AND LAUGHTER of a
man who sounds like the Devil. Ichabod
and Gunpowder run faster and faster
until both are hit with a STUNNING
LIGHT. Ichabod looks into the light,
sees something beyond frightening, and
SCREAMS LOUDER THAN HE OR ANY HUMAN HAS
EVER SCREAMED BEFORE!

The LIGHTS GO TO BLACK. The scream and
the noises stop. The MUSIC continues,
until if finally reaches a crescendo,
and also stops.

LIGHTS UP on the Gossips. Emma sits
transfixed. After a moment, she speaks.

EMMA
What did he see?

MILLY
I'm speculatin', remember...

EMMA
So speculate! What did he see?

MILLY
I think...he thought...he saw...a head.

EMMA
A head?

MILLY
A flyin' head. Comin' right at him.

EMMA
A flyin' head...

KATE
I think you're right. For a change.

EMMA
The Headless Horseman!

                              MILLY
I said that's what HE thought. We all know what was out
there.

                              Center stage, the LIGHTS BEGIN TO COME
                              UP on a pile of smashed pumpkin.

                              KATE
The pumpkin.

                              MILLY
The smashed pumpkin.

                              EMMA
But...where did it come from?

                              MILLY
                    (beat)
I ain't tellin' her.

                              KATE
Well, I ain't tellin' her...

                              EMMA
                    (a revelation)
Ah! Brom...

                              KATE
                    (stopping her)
Uh uh! Don't be castin' aspersions...

                              EMMA
I don't even know what aspersions is...

                              KATE
Neither does she, but that never stopped her.

                              MILLY
But nobody's seen him since. I think...

                              KATE
We know what you think.
                    (sarcastically)
Murder...

                              MILLY
All right, you come up with a different idea...I mean, the
man never come back for his hat! A week now, since the
sociable. A man will always come back for his hat! Unless
he's murdered...

                              Out of the shadows, Ichabod, carrying
                              his satchel, walks toward the pile of
                              smashed pumpkin as the ladies keep
                              arguing.

They adlib an argument about murder and other theories on the matter, as the LIGHTS FADE on them.

Ichabod arrives at the pile of smashed pumpkin, reaches down in the middle of it, and pulls out his hat. He places the hat on his head, and looks to the skies.

ICHABOD
It takes more than a pumpkin to kill a teacher!

Proudly, he hoists his satchel, and walks away.

LIGHTS FADE TO BLACK

END OF PLAY

THE CRITICS RESPOND TO JACK NEARY'S PLAYS

TRICK OR TREAT

"TRICK OR TREAT IS A DOMESTIC HORROR SHOW. A LESS
SKILLED PLAYWRIGHT MIGHT HAVE GONE FOR THE OBVIOUS
AND FOCUSED ON MERCY-KILLING AND THE RAVAGES OF
ALZHEIMER'S. BUT, WITH THE SURPRISING DOINGS OF THE
SECOND ACT, NEARY TAKES AN UNPREDICTABLE DIRECTION...
FAMILY UBER ALLES. ITS SECRETS ARE SUPPOSED TO
PROTECT, BUT THEY ALWAYS COME BACK WITH BITE,
FOLLOWED BY UNIMAGINED CONSEQUENCES. DRAMATIST ARTHUR
MILLER SAID THAT TRAGEDY WAS WHEN THE CHICKENS COME
HOME TO ROOST. AND THE BIRDS ARE ALWAYS IN FLIGHT —
EVEN ON HALLOWEEN." *ARTSFUSE*.

"JACK NEARY'S TRICK OR TREAT MIXES MURDEROUS FAMILY
SECRETS WITH MYSTERY AND COMEDY, INDEED BLACK COMEDY,
THAT PACKS A WALLOP. NORTHERN STAGE PRESENTS A
TAUGHT, RIVETING AND DEEPLY FUNNY AND TOUCHING WORLD
PREMIERE PRODUCTION OF TRICK OR TREAT,... TAUT, ON-THE-
EDGE-OF-YOUR-SEAT STORYTELLING ENRICHED BY REAL
HUMANNESS, AND WITH PLENTY OF WIT... ENTERTAINING AND
DEEPLY AFFECTING." *RUTLAND HERALD*

"TRICK OR TREAT AT NORTHERN STAGE IS A SHOW THAT
WEAVES TOGETHER COMEDY, DRAMA AND SUSPENSE... THE STORY
IS PROPULSIVE, AND NEITHER DIRECTOR NOR PLAYWRIGHT
PAUSES TO TAP THE BRAKES... IN PLAYWRIGHT NEARY'S
HANDS, THAT'S THE LAUNCHING POINT FOR A COMEDY, NOT A
TRAGEDY. WITHOUT AVOIDING THE DRAMA IN GRIM
CIRCUMSTANCES, THE PRODUCTION PAINTS A COMIC REALITY,
BUT IT'S NO WHITEWASH OF COMIC RELIEF. AS NEARY'S
CHARACTERS HIT HUMOROUS NOTES, THEY RING TRUE BECAUSE
THEY ARE PEOPLE, NOT PLOT DEVICES... THE BEST LAUGHS IN
THE SHOW ARE CHARACTER DRIVE. CONVINCING CHARACTERS,
NOT WORDPLAY, SPARK THE AUDIENCE'S LAUGHTER AND
EMOTIONAL INVESTMENT...THIS ENSEMBLE SHOWS HOW POWERFUL
THEATER CAN BE, ESPECIALLY WHEN ACTORS DISCOVER
SURPRISES BEFORE OUR EYES." *ALEX BROWN, SEVEN DAYS*

"THE WORLD PREMIERE COMING INTO ITS FINAL WEEKEND AT

NORTHERN STAGE, IN WHITE RIVER JUNCTION, IS CALLED
TRICK OR TREAT, AND IT'S AN EMOTIONAL ROLLER COASTER
RIDE. PLAYWRIGHT JACK NEARY GIVES US A WORKING CLASS
FAMILY TRYING TO HOLD ITSELF TOGETHER. FOR YEARS,
THEY'VE BEEN KEEPING DARK SECRETS FROM EACH OTHER,
AND FROM THE REST OF THE TOWN. ALZHEIMER'S THREATENS
THE LIFE OF THE MATRIARCH IN SOME SURPRISING WAYS.
HER HUSBAND IS TORN BY CONFLICTING FAMILY LOYALTIES
IN WAYS THAT BREAKS HIS HEART - AND OURS. THAT'S
WHERE NEARY FINDS DARK HUMOR, BUT IT'S ALSO WHY,
AFTER I LEFT THE THEATER, I HAD NIGHTMARES. TO ME, A
SIXTY-SOMETHING WOMAN, THIS BEAUTIFULLY PERFORMED
PLAY WAS MORE TERRIFYING THAN ANY NEWS I'D READ THAT
WEEK. IT'S A TIMELY REMINDER THAT I - OR SOMEONE I
LOVE - COULD FALL PREY TO A STEALTHY, INCURABLE
DISEASE THAT STRIKES SOMEONE IN THE U.S. EVERY SIX
SECONDS." *VERMONT PUBLIC RADIO*

AULD LANG SYNE

WINNER OF 5 NHTA AWARDS RESULTING FROM THE
PETERBOROUGH PLAYERS 2012 PRODUCTION WHICH FEATURED
NYPD BLUE'S GORDON CLAPP

"IT IS A STORY OF TWO VULNERABLE PEOPLE BROUGHT
TOGETHER UNDER VERY STRANGE CIRCUMSTANCES WHO FORM AN
UNLIKELY BOND BASED ON SHARED EXPERIENCE WHO, IN THE
PROCESS, TEACH EACH OTHER HOW TO LIVE. MORE CANNOT BE
REVEALED, BECAUSE THE STORY'S STRENGTH LIES IN ITS
SURPRISES. BUT WHAT CAN BE REVEALED IS ALTHOUGH JOE
AND MARY'S INTERACTIONS ARE ENTERTAINING, THE PLAY
DEALS WITH MANY SERIOUS THEMES - LIFE AND DEATH,
HEAVEN AND HELL - BUT IN SUCH A WAY THAT YOU CAN'T
HELP BUT SIT BACK AND ENJOY THE RIDE - UNTIL THE BALL
DROPS IN TIMES SQUARE." *KEENE SENTINEL, KEENE NH*

"WITH AULD LANG SYNE, NEW CENTURY THEATRE CO-FOUNDER
JACK NEARY HAS WRITTEN A WITTY, ENGAGING, THOUGHTFUL
PLAY THAT PROVIDES FOR A DELIGHTFUL EVENING OF
THEATRE. THE PLAY BEGINS WITH A RAT-A-TAT OPENING
THAT SEEMS RIGHT OUT OF THE BEST OF ABBOTT AND
COSTELLO, WITH SILLY WORDPLAY AND MISUNDERSTOOD
DOUBLE MEANINGS. BUT UNDER NEARY'S SURE WRITING THIS
EVENTUALLY EVOLVES INTO SOMETHING MORE - AN
UNEXPECTED, BUT NOT OUT OF PLACE, EXPLORATION OF
QUESTIONS SUCH AS THE RELATIVE MERITS OF HEAVEN AND
HELL, THE EXISTENCE OF GOD, AND WHAT MAKES LIFE WORTH
LIVING - OR NOT." *IN THE SPOTLIGHT, SPRINGFIELD, MA*

FIRST NIGHT

"A LOVELY RIFF OF MAGIC...TOUCH IT FOR YOURSELF."
KEVIN KELLY, THE BOSTON GLOBE

"NEARY IS A PRO AT RIB-TICKLING; SNAPPY ONE-LINERS
POP FROM HIS PEN LIKE FIRECRACKERS...FIRST NIGHT
DEMONSTRATES THAT NEARY LOVES AND UNDERSTANDS THE
WAYWARD WORKINGS OR ORDINARY PEOPLE'S MINDS AND
HEARTS. HIS HUMOR CARESSES HIS SUBJECTS, NEVER WAGS A
FINGER AT THEM." *ARTHUR FRIEDMAN, THE BOSTON HERALD*

"WHAT A DELIGHT!...JUST AS FRED ASTAIRE WAS ABLE TO
DANCE WITH A HATRACK AND MAKE IT LOOK GOOD, SO
PLAYWRIGHT JACK NEARY IS ABLE TO SIDESTEP THE CLICHÉS
AND FIND THE HUMOR AND THE HEART IN THIS TOUCHING
LITTLE ENCOUNTER." *THE LOS ANGELES TIMES*

"FIRST NIGHT HAS CONSIDERABLE CHARM, ZEST,
IMAGINATION AND EXPERTISE." *VARIETY*

TO FORGIVE, DIVINE

"NEARY IS A CATHOLIC NEIL SIMON. (HE) ADROITLY
BALANCES LAUGHTER AND PATHOS IN A STORY WHOSE ENDING
IS LOVELY, SENSIBLE AND SATISFYING." *ARTHUR FRIEDMAN,
THE BOSTON HERALD"*

"HILARIOUS AND TOUCHING. NEARY HAS AN EAR FOR ONE-
LINERS AND COLLOQUIAL LANGUAGE. IT'S LIKE 'THE BIG
CHILL IN THE CHURCH." *PATTI HARTIGAN, THE BOSTON
GLOBE"*

"NEARY HAS A FLAIR FOR LIVELY, OFTEN FUNNY
DIALOGUE..." *VARIETY*

"WHILE THE HUMOR IN TO FORGIVE, DIVINE HAS A CATHOLIC
BASE, IT IS UNIVERSAL ENOUGH TO APPEAL TO ALL
AUDIENCES BECAUSE ITS THEME OF RECONCILIATION REACHES
BEYOND A SINGLE CREED. NEARY ISN'T SO MUCH INTERESTED
IN LAMBASTING THE CHURCH FOR ITS SHORTCOMINGS AS HE
IS IN DEPICTING THE ROLE THAT IT PLAYS IN ITS
CHARACTERS' LIVES." *CLIFF GALLO, THE LOS ANGELES
READER.*

JERRY FINNEGAN'S SISTER

"... A RICH AND ENDEARING STORY OF A YOUNG MAN'S INFATUATION...THERE IS NOT ONE FALSE NOTE IN NEARY'S VOICE AS PLAYWRIGHT...SEARCH YOUR EXPERIENCE. THIS STORY COULD GO ANYWHERE, RIGHT? IT DOES. IT COMES BACK TO A SIMPLE QUESTION, THOUGH. WILL BRIAN EVER ASK BETH OUT? THE PLAY'S ENDING IS, HANDS-DOWN, THE BEST I'VE SEEN IN SUCH COMEDIES. JERRY FINNEGAN'S SISTER MAKES YOU WONDER HOW ROMANCE EVER WORKS. THEN YOU BELIEVE THERE IS LITTLE ELSE." *LARRY PARNASS, DAILY HAMPSHIRE GAZETTE, NORTHAMPTON, MASSACHUSETTS*

"ONLY A SMALL NUMBER OF PEOPLE HAVE BEEN FORTUNATE ENOUGH TO ESCAPE THE ANGUISH, EMBARRASSMENT AND SELF-RECRIMINATION INVOLVED WITH UNREQUITED LOVE. THESE FEW PEOPLE MAY SYMPATHIZE, BUT WILL NOT EMPATHIZE WITH THE REST OF US WHO HAVE. THOSE WHO HAVE SUFFERED THIS AFFLICTION NEED TO SEE JACK NEARY'S PLAY, JERRY FINNEGAN'S SISTER, IN ORDER TO RELIVE THAT EXPERIENCE IN THE COMPANY OF KIN AND KIND FOR A CATHARSIS OF LAUGHTER AND TEARS." *TIMES HERALD-RECORD, STONY POINT, NY*

THE PORCH

"THE PORCH IS TO EASTERN MASSACHUSETTS WHAT STEEL MAGNOLIAS IS TO NORTHWEST LOUISIANA. A DECEPTIVELY TENDER PLAY THAT IS ALSO VERY FUNNY. IT'S AN INVITING PLACE TO SET A WHILE AND WILL LEAVE YOU FEELING RIGHT NEIGHBORLY." *BROADWAY WORLD*

"THE PORCH IS A PLAY THAT WILL APPEAL TO JUST ABOUT EVERYONE, INCLUDING PEOPLE WHO NORMALLY WOULDN'T GO TO THE THEATER. YOU CAN EVEN SAFELY DRAG YOUR HUSBAND OR FATHER TO THIS PLAY, AND COUNT ON THE FACT THAT HE'LL LEAVE WITH A SMILE ON HIS FACE." *WORDPRESS*

"JACK NEARY'S THE PORCH IS EVERYTHING THEATRE SHOULD BE. IT IS ENDEARING, DROP-DEAD FUNNY, HEARTBREAKING AND, IN THE END, TRIUMPHANT. I LEFT THE THEATER THINKING TO MYSELF, GEE, I WISH I'D WRITTEN THAT." *DICK FLAVIN, EMMY-WINNING AUTHOR AND HUMORIST*

KONG'S NIGHT OUT

"KONG'S NIGHT OUT WILL GIVE YOU TWO HOURS OF HEARTY LAUGHTER, A VISIT FROM AN ENORMOUS GORILLA, AND A BIG SMILE ON YOUR FACE AS YOU LEAVE THE THEATRE!

LAUGHTER ABOUNDS IN THIS SCREWBALL COMEDY!"
BOSTON METRO

"KONG'S NIGHT OUT OFFERS GIGANTIC LAUGHS! A
SUCCULENT THEATRICAL TREAT! DON'T MISS THIS ONE!"
PATRIOT LEDGERS

"KONG-SIZED FUN AND HILARITY!" *BAY WINDOWS, BOSTON*

"MONKEY BUSINESS RULES IN <u>KONG'S NIGHT OUT</u>, A ROWDY
NEW FARCE BY JACK NEARY...A FUNNY PLAY WITH A FUTURE
IN THE REGIONAL, OR EVEN OFF-BROADWAY MARKET!" *LOWELL
SUN*

FRANKENSTEIN

"IT SAYS SOMETHING ABOUT THIS STORY'S APPEAL, AND
WRITER/DIRECTOR JACK NEARY'S GENIUS, THAT WE CAN KNOW
SO MUCH ABOUT WHAT WILL HAPPEN AND YET SIT
MESMERIZED, WAITING FOR THE HORROR TO WIDEN IN THE
DARKNESS. NEARY DOES MORE THAN ADAPT THE STORY MARY
SHELLEY WROTE AS A PRECOCIOUS IF MORBID TEENAGER IN
1818. HE RE-IMAGINES ITS SETTINGS AND LANGUAGE,
TEASING OUT ITS CONUNDRUMS OF SPIRITUALITY AND
EXISTENCE. NEARY KEEPS IT INTERESTING, AND KEEPS THE
HORROR HORRID, BY LIGHTENING THE PLAY'S MANY QUICK
SCENES (THERE ARE 40-ODD SHORT ONES, MOVIE-STYLE)
WITH HUMOR, GALLOWS AND OTHERWISE." *LARRY PARNASS,
DAILY HAMPSHIRE GAZETTE*

THE TURN OF THE SCREW

"A SPINE-TINGLING DRAMA, PUNCTUATED WITH HEART-
STOPPING MOMENTS, LAUNCHES THE SUMMER THEATER SEASON.
JACK NEARY'S ADAPTATION AND EXPERT DIRECTION OF HENRY
JAMES' EERIE <u>THE TURN OF THE SCREW</u> IS A PSYCHOLOGICAL
THRILLER THAT POSES MORE QUESTIONS THAN IT ANSWERS.
THIS GHOST STORY GIVES AUDIENCES MORE THAN THEY
BARGAINED FOR. MOVE OVER STEPHEN KING." *IN THE
SPOTLIGHT, SORINGFIELD, MA*

"...THE SPECTER OF GHOSTS WANDERING THE GROUNDS HAUNTS
EVERYONE AND BUILDS TO A STIRRING AND DISTURBING
CLIMAX...THE EERINESS IS PALPABLE...AN EVENING'S WORTH OF
STARTLES, SPINE-TINGLES AND A CLIMAX OF ABSOLUTE
HORROR...BE PREPARED TO BE SCARED." *DAILY HAMPSHIRE
GAZETTE*

978-853-9620

jack@jacknearyonline.com

www.jacknearyonline.com

Made in the USA
Middletown, DE
15 July 2021

44207054R00060